THE ART OF
ANCESTOR HUNTING

The Art
of
ANCESTOR HUNTING

A Guide to Ancestral Research
and Genealogy

by

OSCAR FRANK STETSON

He who careth not whither he goeth,
careth not whence he came.

17061

STEPHEN DAYE PRESS · PUBLISHERS
NEW YORK

All blank forms recommended in this book, with the exception of those for which credit is given other publishers, are published by Stephen Daye Press and may be purchased from them. A descriptive catalogue is available.

Dedicated to
Myron Thomas Pritchard, Litt. D.

Scholar
Educator
Philosopher
Friend

Whose inspiring advice and criticism
helped produce this book.

CONTENTS

I

FAMILY RECORDS

CHAPTER I. PAGE 13
Introduction

CHAPTER II. PAGE 22
Sources of Information

II

ANCESTRAL RECORDS

CHAPTER I. PAGE 75
Introduction

CHAPTER II. PAGE 81
Charts

CHAPTER III. PAGE 87
Forms

CHAPTER IV. PAGE 111
Items

CHAPTER V. PAGE 117
System

III

GENEALOGICAL RECORDS

CHAPTER I. PAGE 129
Introduction

CHAPTER II. PAGE 135
Scope

CHAPTER III. PAGE 145
General

CHAPTER IV. PAGE 162
Working Papers

CHAPTER V. PAGE 202
Problems

IV

PUBLICATION

CHAPTER I. PAGE 225
Introduction

CHAPTER II. PAGE 230
Preparing Copy

CHAPTER III. PAGE 247
The Book

CHAPTER IV. PAGE 253
Quarterlies

CHAPTER V. PAGE 262
Financing

I

Family Records

CHAPTER ONE: *INTRODUCTION*

THERE is no more fascinating subject in which a person may become occupied than an examination into the history of his ancestry. The study of human beings is an interesting one, especially when they are the particular human beings from whom the student has derived his existence, his character, his likes and dislikes, and those elements which differentiate him from every other human being and constitute him an entity with an individuality.

A large number of people are becoming increasingly interested in the study of their ancestry. Persons everywhere are inquiring as to who were their progenitors, when they came to America, where in this country they settled, in what direction they followed the tide of migration as it moved into new settlements in early days, what they accomplished in business, in education, in public service, what place they occupied in the development of the state and the nation, who their children were and what became of them, and so on with many questions, the answers to which are an engrossing study.

The business of answering these questions has become a profession and many persons are following it with more or less success. To them, however, it is purely a business. There is nothing about it which vitally concerns them except the wages derived therefrom.

There are also many persons taking up this work who have no intention of becoming professional genealogists or making the study a vocation. They seek to answer their own questions and desire the sport connected with the search, and have come to realize that finding one's ancestors and learning to know them intimately through records and history cannot produce its greatest enjoyment if it is to be accomplished through a third and disinterested party. Like many of the pleasures of life, ancestor hunting must be experienced first hand if it is to possess real charm.

To many people the search for ancestors and family connections cannot be prosecuted through the hired worker because of the amount of money involved in the transaction. Family research is a great gamble. Sometimes a few hours work will produce marvelous results and at other times, days, weeks, and sometimes months will be consumed with very little accomplishment to show for the work done. When the search is being paid for by the hour it is often very discouraging and unless a person is financially able to spend considerable money it may prove a disappointing business.

Many people with a keen interest in their progenitors and a longing to know more about them make no move to satisfy their wishes or answer the questions which arise concerning such matters. This is because they are fairly well convinced that they cannot afford to hire the work done and that they do not possess the ability to do it themselves.

THE PURPOSE OF THE BOOK

With that situation in mind this book is prepared:

1st. To bring to the attention of people the desirability of undertaking ancestral and genealogical research, and to show them the enjoyment that is to be derived in doing it—the pleasure there is in living over with the forefathers in family connection their lives of adventure, toil and accomplishment. The satisfaction of seeing themselves as their lives reflect the lives of others who have transmitted to them by blood something of strength and of weakness, of character and the peculiarities of human nature. To understand the lives of today in the light of the lives of yesterday, and to interpret the characters of yesterday in those of today.

2nd. To show to the interested person of average mental ability how very easy it is to do such research work himself, thereby satisfying his longings and answering his ancestral questions himself without any considerable outlay of money, and at the same time opening an avenue of activity from which he will derive the keen enjoyment which always accompanies this sort of work. To take the novice step by step from the very beginning of his ancestral queries through the various phases of the search until he can solve his ancestral problems as successfully as could the professional genealogist. To outline a plan of both genealogical and ancestral research and to work it out to the result of producing either an ancestral history or a genealogy, whichever it is that he assays to accomplish.

CLASSES OF WORK

The study of the history of a family may properly be divided into two distinct branches:

1st. Those who are studying from an ancestral point of view which is the history of a portion of many families converging in one person in the present, usually the student himself, and,

2nd. Those who are studying from a genealogical point of view which is the history of many families diverging from one ancestor at some distant point of time.

The former is a very easy and simple proposition and one that any person with ordinary intelligence may undertake without special training or preparation with a fair expectation of reaching successful results. The latter demands more training and skill if success is to be obtained. With proper introduction to the work and guidance, however, the layman need not hesitate taking up the construction of a genealogy confident of producing a creditable piece of work which will find its place among family histories of the first class.

In this treatise it is purposed:

1st. To discuss those subjects which are common both to ancestral and to genealogical work.

2nd. To treat of those subjects which bear distinctly on the construction of ancestral charts and histories which are not prepared with a view of publication and whose readers will be limited to those individuals having a personal interest in its production, and

3rd. To consider those matters which have to do with the preparation of a genealogy which it is intended shall be published and become a source of information for the general public.

Terminology
Ancestral Charts

An Ancestral Chart is a picture or diagram of a descendant and his ancestors. It is the framework or skeleton on which a Family History is built. It may be arranged in any one of a multitude of ways, sometimes resembling an open fan, but more often shown by a plain diagram on one or more sheets of paper ruled for the purpose and indicating the multiplication of lines necessary to represent the geometrical progression needed to accommodate the actual number of ancestors of any one person.

An Ancestral Chart will contain only names, dates of births, deaths and marriages, and possibly the place of residence of the various people named. It is a skeleton history giving only the vital record.

Ancestral History

An Ancestral History in a compilation of data combined with interesting incidents, with reference to lines of ascent from a common descendant. It starts with a person in the present or some recent time and works back to earlier dates along all lines of blood which have contributed to the life of the individual selected as the starting point, thus embracing many families of different surnames and many strains of blood in no way connected only as they are the ancestors of a common offspring. For instance, assuming that the compiler is taking himself as a starting point, his father and his mother will develop the first division into two distinct family blood lines. Their blood ties are in no way connected only as they merge to become his parents. With the next preceding generation his grandparents will introduce four blood strains by the same process. The compiler is not interested in any of the other children of his grandparents or their families. Ancestral History is one straight line from child to parent so far back as it is carried.

An Ancestral History may end with the emigrant ancestors or it may extend to earlier dates and embrace ancestors prior to emigration to this country.

It is the history of a descendant and his ancestors, and is the direct opposite of a genealogy in that it treats of many totally disconnected families and blood strains brought together in one common descendant, while the genealogy treats of one family and blood strain spread out into a multitude of descendants.

An Ancestral History, because its focal point is in one person of recent date, or at most in one family of brothers and sisters, is of a more private nature than a genealogy. It is of interest in its totality to only a few people and is prepared more for a pastime than for any historical value it may reveal and, therefore, is not prepared with a view of publication.

Introduction

Genealogy

A Genealogy is a compilation of data with reference to lines of descent. It starts with one common ancestor who may be the emigrant, or one of the emigrants if there were several bearing the same surname, who came to this country in colonial times. Or it may begin with any subsequent ancestor heading a particular branch of the family surname. For instance, Matthew Cushing with wife, Nazareth, and sons, Daniel, Jeremiah, Matthew and John and Daughter, Deborah, came to America in the ship "Diligent" in 1638. A genealogy of the Cushing family may include this entire family and their descendants, or it may be the Daniel Cushing genealogy treating only of Daniel, son of Matthew and Nazareth, and his descendants.

From the beginning point, wherever it may be, the genealogy works down to a more recent date, even to the present time enumerating by generations the descendants of the selected ancestor and following only the blood lines of the one chosen forefather. For instance, if the compiler is preparing the genealogy of the family of his own surname, i.e. of his father's side, he will only be concerned with the history of his mother to the extent of naming her as the wife of his father and the mother of the children having that father's blood, with the vital record of her birth, death and marriage to his father, and the names of her parents. She has no further part in the genealogy of her husband's family. Of the four grandparents the only one with whom he is concerned is the father of his father who bears the same surname, and that grandfather's wife to the same extent to which he carried his father's wife, his own mother, and, while all the other grandparents are dropped and ignored, it is the purpose of the genealogy to deal with all the offspring of the one grandfather who is picked up in the blood line of the ancestral name and carry them to some point where it has been determined to drop out those who have changed their surname by marriage. Genealogy is a history of one family of one blood strain only.

The genealogy may be restricted to those persons bearing the same surname as the selected ancestor in which case it is only the history of sons and unmarried daughters of the family, or it may be enlarged to include the marriages of daughters and the enumeration of their immediate families, which by the way is the most common practice and the plan to be most strongly recommended, or it may be still further extended to include all known descendants of the ancestor, thus embracing the ancestral name and the surnames acquired by the daughters through marriage in all branches.

The latter method would produce a family history which could be termed a full genealogy and would be the complete history so far as it could be gathered of an ancestor and all his blood descendants—the complete history of one strain of blood. Thus, while an Ancestral History is the history of a descendant and his ancestors, a Genealogy is a history of an ancestor and his descendants.

The Genealogy has an interest for a large number of people; it will embrace many who are connected by blood ties to the common ancestor, and also students in its many branches. It is, therefore, prepared with a view of publication that it may fully serve its purpose, reach the attention of those interested in its record, and justify the expense of its compilation.

Introduction

Genealogist   A Genealogist is a person who, professionally or otherwise, practices the science of examining public and private records with the object of compiling in some form the history of a family. In its broader meaning it embraces both those persons who are working on Genealogies and those who are preparing Ancestral Charts and Ancestral Histories. In this treatise the term Genealogist will be used in its broader sense to indicate any person who for any reason is examining and compiling any sort of family records.

CHAPTER TWO: *SOURCES OF INFORMATION*

THE question most frequently asked by the laity and the person who is contemplating ancestral or genealogical work is where to search and find material regarding family history. The answer to this question requires much thought for it is the crux of the whole matter. If sufficient information can be found the preparation of an Ancestral History or a Genealogy is only a matter of editorial work, and if the data cannot be found all the literary and editorial ability in the world cannot produce a family history. To insure success, family facts must be found. Considered as one problem the task seems enormous, but really in the last analysis it is the simple plan of doing only one thing at a time and allowing the accomplished work to suggest the next step to be taken.

In ancestral work the problem of tracing the family lines is largely one for the individual worker. He is jumping with such rapidity from one line or one family to another entirely disassociated that he cannot well interest any one else in his problems. Then, too, he is working with so many individual lines that it is probable that he can find much of his material in printed genealogies of the various families with which he is concerned. He is not working for publication and anything that he can find he may feel free to appropriate for his own compilation without question of plagiarism. Not infrequently he may be able to copy or abstract from a printed genealogy a long line of ancestors in some one of the families from which he is descended. In that case his task is merely one of abstraction and arrangement in its proper place, in his history or on his chart.

For the Ancestral History it is an easy matter to race back over the printed books which may be found on the shelves of Genealogical Libraries and copy from them such bits as may be desired for the search in hand.

When this has been done, however, the real work of collecting data begins. Then must be brought into action some or all of the methods of securing information which will be discussed in this chapter, as it applies to ancestral and genealogical work alike.

In genealogical work the problem is somewhat different. The project is of interest to many people of many branches of the family and members of those branches will be interested to help with the work. Then, too, various printed genealogies will not be found, or if found, will not be of so great assistance, for only one family is under consideration. If there were recently printed genealogies of that family there would be no need for the work of preparing another. Therefore there must necessarily be gathered much more information from original sources.

In examining all sources of information, whether published or original, the examiner should bear in mind that there are often changes of surnames. These changes occurred usually in the early generations and probably were most often occasioned by the limited education of the times. They were changed sometimes for euphony and not infrequently for no apparent reason at all. No attention will be given here to the development of surnames from the time of William the Conqueror when he conferred them on his subjects, until the settlement of America, as those changes have no part in the preparation of an American genealogy other than in its introductory chapter which will ordinarily be furnished by some English genealogist or examiner experienced in the profession.

In the search for Ancestral History if the examiner wishes to pursue the study beyond the point covered in the introduction to the various genealogies which he has occasion to use he should consult some good authority in the matter.

Many old English names have not been changed since their early use, as for instance Stone, Cushing, etc. Others have had a variety of spellings but have always kept to the same general sound, such as Josselyn-Joslin-Joclyn. In other instances still greater change is noted as in Whiton-Whiting, Stodder-Stoddard and Linkhorn-Lincoln. In some instances various spellings have been retained by different branches of the family as Crooker and Crocker both of which have descended from the same original name. Sometimes these various spellings were used interchangeably as Munroe-Munro-Monroe all of which forms have continued in different lines of the family down to the present time. Many of them were definite changes as in the Linkhorn-Lincoln name, the old form having entirely disappeared.

The genealogist will find a family by the name of Stodder moving out of one town and becoming Stoddard upon their entry into another town. This indicates that in histories and records all similar names should be examined, and especially if the family is lost by their change of town residence.

Phonetic spelling had its strong advocates in early town clerks, but it is suspected that they knew no better rather than that any orthographical principle was involved.

PRINTED SOURCES OF INFORMATION

1. Genealogies and How to Use Them

There is so much individuality displayed in printed genealogies that it is somewhat difficult to set down any general rule governing their use. Usually, however, one of two numbering plans is employed by the genealogical writer.

The first, and by far the most common practice, is to number consecutively from *1*, representing the emigrant ancestor, to as high a number as is found necessary for the completion of the work. This is the plan recommended by the New England Historic Genealogical Society and is usually designated by its name, and may be explained thus:

The emigrant or beginning ancestor is numbered *1*, which constitutes the first generation, his oldest child is numbered *2*, the next child *3*, and so on throughout the family. If he had ten children the tenth child would be numbered *11*, *1* having been used for the father, and these ten children would constitute the second generation.

Assuming the oldest child to have been a son with a family, he would be the first one to be picked up and carried on. When he was picked up for further consideration the same number would be given him that was previously assigned to him in the list of his father's children, i.e. *2*, and his first child would be numbered *12* which would be the first unused number, and so on progressively throughout his family. If he had twelve children his *12th* child would be numbered *23*. The next family to be given consideration in the book would be that of the next child of the emigrant's family to be picked up and carried on. Assuming that the second child was a daughter who died during her minority and did not marry she was therefore dropped. The third child of the emigrant may have been a son who married and had five children. He would therefore be the next to claim consideration. He would be given his previous number of *4* and his first child would be numbered *24* and his last child *28*. This plan would be continued throughout the book, running the numbers into thousands if necessary.

It is, briefly, giving the common ancestor the number *1* and adding the next unused number for each person of the blood named until the end of the book is reached, using the first number assigned to the child carried forward when he is again picked up later as the head of a family in his own generation.

By this method if it is desired to back up the line of any particular person it is necessary to look up each generation, stepping back from one generation to that preceding it, and there is no way of comparing descendants from any specific ancestor.

It is not uncommon in this system to find a genealogist who in practice has omitted the numbers of those persons who were not picked up for further consideration. By this method something is saved in the use of large numbers, and if this plan were adopted by a genealogist it would be found in the illustration above that the second child of the ancestor, who was a daughter, unmarried and dying before reaching maturity, would have no number and the following child would be numbered *3* instead of *4*. There is very little to be said for or against this modification of the plan. Where every child is given a number it is common practice to place a plus sign or an asterisk in front of the numbers indicating those who will be considered later in the book.

The other plan of numbering most often found is that adopted by the compiler of the Chapin Genealogy where numbers are used, and by Mr. Waldo Lincoln in the Lincoln and the Waldo genealogies where letters are used. It may be described by quoting from Mr. Lincoln's introduction to the *Lincoln Genealogy* as follows:

"The earliest emigrant of the family, in this case Samuel Lincoln, is lettered *a*, his children are lettered *aa*, *ab*, *ac*, etc. The children of the oldest child are lettered *aaa*, *aab*, *aac*, etc., of the second child *aba*, *abb*, *abc*, etc. and so on through each succeeding generation, each descendant having as many letters as the generation to which he belongs, and letters showing exactly his line of descent.

For example, take the last name in this volume (Lincoln Genealogy), *Mordacai Abel Lincoln, adaaa bbcgb*. For convenience in counting, a space corresponding to a decimal point is left after the fifth and tenth letters. There being ten letters, he belongs to the tenth generation and is descended from *ad*, the fourth child of *Samuel, a*. To look up any of his ancestors it is only necessary to leave off a sufficient number of letters and to turn to the person indicated by those remaining without resorting to the index or the intervening ancestors. For instance, to learn the record of his great-grandfather, leave off the last three letters, *cgb*, and there is left *adaaa bb*, which is the index letter of Thomas Lincoln. Take now the index letters of *President Lincoln, adaaa db*, and it is clear he and the aforesaid Thomas were own cousins, the first five letters showing that they had the same grandfather.

In the case of children, to save space, only the final letters are used and to obtain their full index letters it is necessary to affix the final index letter of each child to the index letters of the parent. For instance, see *Deborah Lincoln*, *aabab*, her oldest child, John, is that of his mother, *aabab*, with the addition of his own letter, *a*, making his complete index letters *aabab a*."

The *Chapin Genealogy* follows the same general plan with the use of figures instead of letters. The children of the emigrant ancestor are numbered *1-1*, *1-2*, *1-3*, etc., the third generation being numbered *1-1-1*, *1-1-2*, *1-1-3*, etc. In the figure plan there is only room for the insertion of ten children without running into the complication of the eleventh child being read either as *11* or *1-1* which would throw the child off one generation. This means that the figures have to be hyphenated. Thus the person lettered by Mr. Lincoln's plan *adaaa bbcg* would have to be numbered by the Chapin plan *1-4-1-1-1-2-2-3-7*.

Nothing is to be said in the description of the two plans as to the merits or demerits of either. In a later chapter this matter will receive attention with methods of use. The point here is to assist the searcher in the use of what others have done.

In ancestral work an examination of the index for the name nearest in line of the person about whom the examination is centering will show the beginning place where the book will be of assistance. If the name of the immediate ancestor is not found, that of the next earlier generation should be sought. For example, if the examiner whose name is James West, son of Thomas West, knows that his grandfather West was named Samuel, he should first look in the index for a Thomas whom he can identify by the dates, marriage etc. as his father. Failing to find him, he should then search for a Samuel whom he can identify as his grandfather, and so the search should be continued until an ancestor is found in some generation who can be identified in the line.

Having found a starting place in the book the examiner will find set against the name, if the consecutive numbering plan explained above is used, a number, perhaps *347*. He will then turn back in the book until he finds the same number against the same name in a list of children. This will not be difficult, as numbers are in sequence. Glancing at the father of this list of children he will note that he is numbered, perhaps *264*. He will then repeat his process of turning back to find *264*, and so on until he reaches the person who is numbered *1* and is the progenitor about whom that genealogy is written. This is termed "backing up the book," or "backing up the line."

Thus the examiner will skip from back to front of the book and abstract what he wants for those families in direct line of ancestry, or having noted the line he may begin at the person numbered *1* and abstract forward to where his line is dropped, or in the case of a female ancestor, is merged by marriage, thus rendering the balance of the book of no interest in that particular search.

The second method of numbering described as having been used by Mr. Lincoln with its variation as in the *Chapin Genealogy* will be followed in the same way from back to front of the book with the exception that with each generation stepped back the last letter or number on the right-hand side of the combination will be dropped. For example if James West is *1-3-4-5-6-7*, his father, Thomas, will be

1-3-4-5-6, and Samuel will be *1-3-4-5*, and so on back to *1*. If letters are used instead of numbers, the same process of dropping the last letter in each generation stepped back applies.

There are various plans of numbering and arrangement which are original with the compilers of the books in which they are found, and if not original, they are so seldom found in other books that their explanation is not attempted. They are entirely strange to common practice and, while they may have some points to commend them, they will have to be studied carefully by the examiner unless their author has included a description of the plan in the introduction to his work. Some of these plans are freaks, so complex in their detail and scheme that they render the book in which they are found almost useless. Only by the most careful study can they be followed and then with a feeling of suspicion on the part of the examiner that he may be entirely wrong in his interpretation of the plan and erroneous in any findings he may abstract.

For genealogical work the plan of use is entirely different. In that case the examiner is not concerned with his own line only, but with all lines bearing relationship with the family upon whose history he is working. He will seldom find a genealogy in which the surname about which he is building a genealogy will be carried along in the male lines, as that would be a part of his own genealogy. He will find females of the ancestral surname who have married into the family of the surname about which the genealogy he is consulting has been written, and it is of these marriages and their offspring that he will be seeking information. He will, therefore, need to pick up in the index every reference to the surname upon which he is working and abstract the record, carrying his search into collateral lines so far as he has previously decided regarding this point.

2. Town Histories

Hundreds of histories have been published covering the interests of various towns, especially in New England. The larger number of these histories not only cover the historical development of the towns about which they are written, but also contain a section of genealogies of the families which have entered into the life of the town. In the *Weymouth Town History*, for instance, two entire volumes are devoted to genealogies.

These histories usually cover pretty thoroughly the development of the town along various educational, religious, civic and industrial lines, and frequently mention is made of those men and their families who have attained prominence in town affairs. In this way can often be found the place and importance of the family in the community.

The genealogical section in these histories is usually arranged alphabetically and ordinarily begins with the advent of the family into the town, with a sketch of the early history in direct line from an emigrant ancestor. They quite carefully give the genealogy of those who spent all or a part of their lives within the confines of the town. And therein is to be found their limitation. For instance, in the *History of Hanover, Massachusetts*, on page 389, is found:

> "William Studley, son of Nathan, married June 10, 1832, Elizabeth C. Haskell, daughter of Jonathan Haskell of Ipswich. They had nine children born in East Abington only TWO of whom we follow."

The History then proceeds to carry along the families of two of the nine children who made their homes in Hanover. This all helps, but it does not account for the other seven children which will be wanted by the compiler of the genealogy, and if they are wanted for ancestral lines the one wanted may be one of the seven who did not live in Hanover and thus this town history is of little use.

However, Hanover says the nine children were born in East Abington, and in the Abington History is found on page 441 the names of all nine children. It will be seen that the Hanover History was valuable as suggesting where further search should be made.

Unlike this, however, may be a reference to a town which has never published its history, or if so, has omitted the genealogical section, in which case the genealogist must resort to other means in following the family.

Families out of New England are not so easily followed by means of town histories, as the custom of printing them has not been so generally prevalent in other sections of the country. Settlements were of more recent date and the need for getting early records into print has not become so apparent. In cases where branches have migrated to the central and mid-western sections of the country, it is usually necessary to work from both ends towards a middle connecting link, running the line in New England until it is lost by removal, then backing up on the various families found in that section of the country to which the migration from the east was supposed to have been made, trusting that thereby a connecting link may be established.

The removals are ordinarily not so early in date as to be

entirely out of memory of some member of the family. Some old person can often be found who will remember hearing his grandparents tell from whence the family came in the east. A good illustration of this is found in the recently published book, *Grandmother Brown's Hundred Years*.

Care should be exercised in the use of town histories to observe the date of publication. Not uncommonly, the brief statement "No children," will be marked against the record of a husband and wife, or only one or two children will be enumerated, when it is known that this family actually did have a number of children. The examination of the date of publication will show that the history was compiled soon after the couple married or during the early years of their married life. What the historian has intended to convey is the fact that at the date of writing he had included such members of the family as then existed. Some of these town histories date back many years to publication. Dean's History of Scituate, Mass., was printed in 1831, and Winsor's History of Duxbury, Mass., was printed in 1849, and they are both exceedingly vague in their genealogies of that date as the following taken from Dean's book will indicate:

> "There was Benoni Studley in Scituate, whose children John, Abigail, Joshua, Gideon, Sarah, and Benoni were born from 1702 to 1723."

Caution should be exercised in following names of towns. When it is written in a Massachusetts history that a certain family removed at an early date to Littleborough, Maine, and it is found that there is no such place in Maine, it must be borne in mind that a great many towns, especially in Maine, have changed their names for one reason or another.

Littleborough, Maine, is now known as Leeds; Port Royal is Livermore, etc. Many towns and localities and even streets which had been named from mother country associations were changed at the time of the Revolutionary War. King and Queen Streets in Bristol, Rhode Island, became at that time Constitution and State Streets. One must not be surprised to read that certain early settlers were given grants of land in Canada to which place they removed with their families, and later find that these grants were in no other place than what are now northern Worcester County towns in Massachusetts where the family was located as having settled on their "Canada Grant."

Lists of many changes in names and lines of towns will be found in the legislative year books and manuals published regularly by many of the states. These books may be secured through the offices of the several Secretaries of State, or through legislators.

Not only were town names changed, but large towns laid out in the early times have been cut up and new names given to those sections created as new towns. Early town records were often carried into the new town rather than being left with the old town. Smithfield, Rhode Island, is one of the older towns of the state, but its early records will be found in the City of Central Falls. They were removed from Smithfield in 1895 when the territory now comprising the City of Central Falls was set off from Lincoln, which in turn had been set off from Smithfield in 1871.

State lines have been shifted and it is found that the early records of that part of the present City of Pawtucket, Rhode Island, lying east of the Seekonk River are with the county records of Bristol County, Massachusetts, the territory having been a part of the old town of Rehoboth, Massachusetts; later known as Pawtucket, Massachusetts, and now Pawtucket, Rhode Island. Thus boundary lines were changed which moved families from one township to another and from one state to another without moving them from the house in which they had lived for years or perhaps for a lifetime.

An interesting situation was recently revealed regarding this point. John Joles was supposed to have been born, to have lived and to have died in Warren, Rhode Island. It was found by the record that he died in Bristol, Rhode Island, an adjoining town. This record greatly disturbed some of his descendants who appealed for help to establish the facts in the case. It was found that the old Warren-Bristol line passed directly through the Joles house which stood not over half a mile south from the center of Warren village, and that the family bedroom where John slept was on the Bristol side of the line. The town line was later moved south one mile leaving the entire house a mile on the Warren side. At the time John died, however, if he died in his bed, he was in Bristol. But if he ate in the old-fashioned kitchen, a custom prevailing in the early days, he ate in Warren. Therefore he doubtless was born and died in Bristol, but lived in Warren all his life, and actually was born, always lived in, and died in the same house and in adjoining rooms.

The obituary of a man who recently died in East Providence, Rhode Island, stated that he died in that town, but that he was born in Seekonk, Massachusetts, and followed the statement by saying that he was born in the house in which he died. This was all true. The record of his birth will be found in Seekonk, Massachusetts, and that of his death in East Providence, Rhode Island, the latter town having been incorporated in 1862 by the settlement of the boundary line between the states of Massachusetts and Rhode Island.

What has been found true in the instances recited will be found in more or less degree in all of the eastern states. These instances will show the necessity of examining records of adjoining towns for data lacking where they supposedly should be found. In consulting town histories this should be borne in mind and histories covering adjoining territory should be examined. The use of a map showing locations and adjoining towns will be helpful.

Regarding the use of town histories as a source of genealogical information it should be remembered that while genealogies proper are usually prepared by some one who had either professional training or the interest of the family uppermost in mind, town histories are frequently prepared in commemoration of some historical anniversary in connection with the town and prepared somewhat sketchily by a number of people whose work is patched together as best it can be, with the result that many and glaring inaccuracies are displayed.

3. Genealogical Indexes

The genealogist will frequently find that there is no published genealogy of the family name and no town history covering the locality where the family was known to have lived. He will find there is no one fund of information and his work will necessarily be built up by gathering here a bit and there a bit and piecing the bits together.

There have been several attempts to gather information of families which is contained in books, pamphlets, histories, genealogies, magazines, etc. into a cumulative index in order that the genealogist may find under the surname in the index what has been published relating to the family. These indexes are exceedingly valuable and are great time savers. They are quite frequently keyed to save space and a small book will be found to contain a surprising amount of information.

One of the newer indexes is that prepared by Donald Lines Jacobus, M.A., published in 1932 from which the following example is quoted to illustrate the general character of the work:

> Hawes, Edmund.   Duxbury   Yarmouth
> A.1. (65-160)   D. (20-73)

By consulting the key it is found that the above means that the *New England Historical and Genealogical Register* (A.1.) volume 65 at page 160, and *The Mayflower Descendant* (D) volume 20 at page 73 will contain information relating to Edmund Hawes who was in Duxbury and Yarmouth.

Of the older indexes which are well known and reliable should be mentioned Munsell's *List of Titles of Genealogical Articles in American Periodicals and Kindred Works* 165 pages, published in 1899, in which information is given in the following form:

> "Sherman, Ancestry of Rev. John Sherman and Capt. John Sherman (of Dedham, Mass.) by a descendant of Capt. John Sherman. New England Hist. and Gen. Register LI (1897) 309-15."

and Derrie's work, also published by Munsell in 1886 and entitled *Alphabetical Index of American Genealogies and Pedigrees*, 245 pages. Both of these are old and of course much has been published to be indexed since they were printed, still they are standard and authentic and by no means should be shunned because of the date of their publication.

Another good work is *Index to American Genealogies and Genealogical Material contained in all Works such as Town Histories, County Histories, Local Histories, Historical Societies, Publications, Biographies, Historical Periodicals and Kindred Works, Alphabetically Arranged.* Its information is shown in the following form:

> LANDON. American Ancestry II 69
> Burleigh's Guild Genealogy 96-8
> Champian Genealogy 390
> New York Gen. and Biog. Rec. XXVIII 24-7
> Va. Mag. of Hist. and Biog. II (1895)
> Wyman, Hist. Genealogy 116

For English ancestry, *Marshall's Genealogical Guide* is recommended. It is also advisable to consult the Catalog of the Library of Congress under the subject of American and English Genealogies.

4. Genealogical Dictionaries

The best known and most used dictionary of genealogy is undoubtedly the one prepared by James Savage, published in four volumes in 1880 and entitled *A Genealogical Dictionary of the First Settlers of New England, Showing Three Generations of those Who Came before May 1692.* Since only three generations are shown, the first of which must have come before 1692 there is no need for recent editions and the original printing of 1860 is as useful as though Mr. Savage had revised to the time of his death. The following is his method of imparting his knowledge:

BENTLEY, John, Charlestown, perhaps s. of William, d. 20 Nov. 1690. Richard, Charlestown in 1690, had w. Margaret. William, a passeng. to Boston 1635 aged 47 in the "True-love," with John, 17, and Alice, 15, perhaps his ch. but where he pich. his tent is unkn. to me, as is also anything a. Mary, a passeng. the same yr. in the "Defence," aged 20. Bentley is a parish in the Deanery of Doncaster and is part of Yorkshire.

In some families Mr. Savage gives very full consideration as is seen from the abstract of the Breck family as follows:

BRECK, Edward, Dorchester 1636, freem. 22 May 1639, came prob. from Ashton in Co. Devon, was an officer of the town 1642, 5, 6 and after, d. 2 or 6 Nov. 1662. Had Robert wh. he brought from Eng.; John; Mary, Bapt 6 Aug. 1648; Eliz. and Susanna. The w. d. 11 Nov. 1653. His wid. Isabel, who was his 2nd w. and had been bef. wid. of John Rigby of D. m. 14 Nov. 1663 Anthony Fisher; Mary m. 9, Jan. 1687 Samuel Paul; Eliz. m. 11 Mar. 1670, John Minot; and Susanna m. 20 Mar. 1674 or 5 John Harris. But he must have had ano. d. for his will of 30 Oct. 1662, only 3 d. bef. his d. ment. d. Elinor."

Thus it will be seen that Savage by the tremendous use of abbreviation crowds a great deal into small space and in his four volumes imparts much information.

Another Dictionary to be recommended is that of John Farmer under the title *A Genealogical Register of the First Settlers of New England, Containing an Alphabetical List of the Governors, Deputy Governors, Assistants or Counsellors, Ministers of the Gospel in the Several Colonies from 1620 to 1692, Representatives of the General Court of Massachusetts from 1634 to 1692, Graduates of Harvard College to 1662, Members of the Ancient and Honorable Artillery Co. to 1662, Freemen Admitted to Massachusetts Colony from 1630 to 1662, With many other Early Inhabitants of New England and Long Island, N. Y. from 1620 to 1675. To which has been added Various Genealogical and Biographical Notes Collected from Ancient Records, Manuscripts and Printed Books.* This work was published in 1829. The following is quoted to show his style of treatment:

> STEWART, Duncan. One of the early settlers of Newbury, d. in Rowley in 1717 ae. 100 yrs. Coffin. John, Springfield in 1654 d. 21 Apr. 1690 (See Stuart). Richard, member of ar. co. 1652.

While this work bears date of over one hundred years ago, it deals only with those settlers from 1620 to 1675 and the date of publication does not greatly matter. The book is still a standard of use.

There is also an index prepared by Charles Henry Pope which is very good. It is much the same as Savage and Farmer. It is entitled *The Pioneers of Massachusetts. A descriptive List Drawn from Records of Colonies, Towns and Churches and other Contemporaneous Documents.* It contains about five hundred pages and was published in 1900.

There is an index for Connecticut published by Royal R. Hinman in 1852 and entitled *A Catalog of the Names of the Early Puritan Settlers of the Colony of Connecticut, with the Time of their Arrival in the Country and Colony; Their Stand-*

ing in Society; Place of Residence; Condition of Life; Where from; Business etc. as far as is Found on Record.

John Osborne Austin's, *The Genealogical Dictionary of Rhode Island. Comprising three Generations of Settlers who came before 1690*, published in 1887, gives the same treatment to the families of Rhode Island which Hinman does for those of Connecticut.

For southern families, Armstrong's *Notable Families* is recommended. The genealogist may also consult *The Handbook of Genealogy*, published by the Genealogical Society of Utah, which may prove helpful.

There are many more books published on this order and with varying degrees of reliability and usefulness which will be found on the shelves of Genealogical Libraries and Historical Societies and which the genealogist will find useful. He should be certain, however, before quoting them or using the information they contain that they are reliable.

5. Genealogical Magazines

The best known of the Genealogical magazines is the *New England Historical and Genealogical Register* which is published by the New England Historic Genealogical Society in Boston. It has reached its ninetieth volume and contains a great fund of genealogical information which has been carefully checked for correctness and is carefully indexed.

Closely following it in importance is the *New York Genealogical and Biographical Record* of which there are sixty-six volumes of valuable matter.

The Essex Institute of Salem, Massachusetts, has published a large historical and genealogical collection of which there are to date over seventy volumes. In the south there are the *Virginia Magazine* and the *William and Mary College Quarterlies* which are good. There are many other publications of the sort, some of them authentic and valuable and some which are not so carefully checked as they might be. It is suggested that before using any work which has not passed the test of accuracy the genealogist inquire from an authority or the librarian of some reliable historical or genealogical society as to its value and authenticity. It is no sure sign because a statement appears as fact that it is indeed so, and caution is advised even where there would seem to be no need for it.

6. Publications of Hereditary Societies

Many of the hereditary societies print the family record of their membership and for the most part they can be relied upon because entrance to the various societies is pretty well guarded. The best known of these publications is the quarterly printed by the Daughters of the American Revolution which has reached its one hundred and twenty-eighth volume. While these records may be relied upon, the information conveyed is largely based upon war records of the Revolution and little of general family history will be found other than lines of descent from those who saw service in that war.

The quarterly of the Mayflower Society printed under the name of *The Mayflower Descendant* like that of the above named society draws its information from one class only, namely the passengers on the Mayflower and deals only with them and their descendants.

The advice regarding the use of the genealogical magazines and quarterlies may well be extended to embrace the publication of the lesser known hereditary society records. They should be relied upon only after the recommendation of some one who is familiar with them and knows their worth.

7. Published Early Vital Records

Some of the states have accumulated and published in whole or in part copies of the vital records prior to the date at which recording by towns and municipalities became obligatory. This has been done in some instances with records prior to 1850 at which time Massachusetts and Rhode Island enacted a law requiring towns and cities to keep a record of births, deaths and marriages. In some of the states the obligatory keeping of vital records is of very much more recent date.

There were spasmodic attempts both by law and by ambitious town and city clerks to keep vital statistics from the very beginning of New England settlements, but officials were lax in this matter and in many instances made no attempt whatever to make the records.

The Eddy Town Record Fund of the New England Historic Genealogical Society has enabled that society to publish for the Commonwealth of Massachusetts the vital records of many of its towns. In these publications authority is given for all records and any variation from different sources is carefully noted. The books constitute a valuable collection of great usefulness. No claim is made as to the completeness of these records. The family doctor may have noted in his diary the birth of two children in a family. The minister may have baptized three children of the same family, the name of only one noted being the same as those mentioned by the physician. The family burial lot may have headstones for a couple more children whose names were not mentioned by either the doctor or the clergyman, and there may have been still others who escaped the physician, baptism and the grave and grew up to rear in their time sizeable families. The compilation of vital statistics will probably get the record of the doctor, the minister and the gravestones, giving each credit for the information furnished.

Nor is there any claim as to the correctness of either names or dates. There is a very successful claim for the correctness in copying what was found, but the copyist could not vouch for what the original record lacked through carelessness or misinformation. It is evident that those who kept diaries in the old days were not very unlike those who keep them now, and the writing was sometimes delayed until the combined efforts of the entire family, called in for assistance, could not fix the correct date or name. It is not surprising to read in the minister's diary that on a certain day he attended the funeral of some one whose death, according to the doctor's diary, did not occur until several days later. Nor must the genealogist be disturbed if he finds the record of a will brought in for probate several days prior to the death of the testator, thus showing that a town clerk did not keep his records written up to date and that either a slip had been made in entering the date of death, or the probate proceedings had been inadvertantly recorded as a part of the business of a session of the court prior to that in which it was actually taken up. All mankind is human, even town clerks.

Allowance must be made for difference in given names and for nicknames. If the doctor was told that the new baby was to be named Sarah, he entered it so in his diary if he entered it at all. If, after thought, it was decided to name the baby after an Aunt Maria, Maria she was baptized, and Maria she will be found, if at all, on the records of the minister or the church. Or it may be that the doctor entered her as Polly and the minister as Mary, and both were correct as Polly was the old nickname for Mary.

What the New England Historic Genealogical Society has done for a part of the Commonwealth of Massachusetts, James N. Arnold, working alone attempted to do for the entire state of Rhode Island. Mr. Arnold's work was published at the expense of the state and is a valuable contribution to published records. The task, however, was too large for one man to accomplish with the care that the work should have received. Mr. Arnold could not in the time at his disposal canvass families for private records or copy inscriptions from cemeteries. The result was that his work is not as complete as the work done in Massachusetts, and the genealogist using his books must not expect to find as complete or as accurate a record as he might desire.

WAR RECORDS

Several of the states have attempted to gather the war records of those men who lived within their bounds and saw service in the American Revolution, that the information of their services might be preserved in orderly fashion. Notable is the work done by the Commonwealth of Massachusetts in its *Soldiers and Sailors of the Revolutionary War* in seventeen large volumes.

It is sometimes difficult to recognize and use the information after it has been found, as is evidenced by a recent search for the record of one Joseph Thompson who was known to have seen service from Massachusetts. It was not known from what section of the Commonwealth he served and the records show twenty-seven Joseph Thompsons who were credited with service during the war. It is a question which, if any one of them, is the particular Joseph who was wanted by the inquirer; and the whole matter is as much a question now as it was before the search was undertaken.

Little has been done with records of the wars subsequent to the Revolution because records of soldiers and sailors in the later wars were more standardized and are more easily ascertained from the files of the various government departments, such as those of the War and Navy and the Pension office at Washington.

STATE AND COUNTY GAZETTEERS

Library shelves are filled with these voluminous works. They are usually published with funds privately solicited and contain biographical and genealogical sketches of varying historical importance which have transpired in the history of the town or county about which they are written. Their real value as a source of genealogical information is rather limited and the examiner for family facts may be disappointed in his use of them.

COURT AND LAND RECORDS

There have been published and distributed for the general use of libraries several sets of books dealing with Colonial court and land records, as for instance, *Probate Records of Essex County Massachusetts* which are a copy of the early probates in that county; and *Suffolk Deeds* which is a set of a dozen of more volumes covering early land transactions in Suffolk County Massachusetts.

There are rich finds in these old records and it is a great convenience if the genealogist can consult them in a near-by library instead of having to travel to Salem or Boston, Massachusetts, to examine the originals. If, after having located what he wants in the transcripts, he desires to see the originals, he knows where he may find that which he seeks and no time or money is wasted in the search. It is a pity that some of the shelf room taken up by "Gazetteers" and "Biographical Sketches" could not be occupied by authentic records of this nature.

BIOGRAPHICAL SKETCHES

A large number of sets of books, usually gotten up with attractive covers and pretty well filled with steel engravings or photogravures have been brought out and are still being published under such titles as "Representative Men of————," "Encyclopedia of Biography," etc. They are printed by private subscription and contain biographical sketches of those persons and their immediate families who subscribe to the publication, the amount of the subscription determining whether or not a photograph is included. The biography is either written by the subject himself and is his estimate of himself and his family, or is prepared by an editor from material furnished by the subject of the sketch.

The "Representative Men" are too frequently those who represent the subscription price without regard to their real worth as biographical characters in their community, and, also, too often there are omitted the biographies of those persons of real worth who should have representation in a work of the sort, but who, because they are not financially interested, are not counted as "Representative Men."

It is needless to say that the only value of these books to the genealogist is in stray genealogical lines which may be found in them and those lines only lead to the subject of the sketch and are by no means a family history. It should also be said that the genealogies contained in these works are quite likely to be a mixture of fact and tradition with no demarcation between the former and the latter.

HERALDRY

The subject of heraldry and coats of arms will be only slightly touched upon. It is a subject sufficient for a treatise in itself and there are many good works on the subject. It is sufficient for the purposes of this textbook to refer to a few standard works and to advise the genealogist, if he wishes to delve deeper into the matter, either to employ an expert on heraldry or secure and study some of the standard textbooks dealing with the subject.

Standard works to be found in any good library having a genealogical department will include John Burke's *Dictionary of the Peerage and Baronetage of the British Empire;* Sir Bernard Burke's *Genealogical and Heraldic History of the Landed Gentry of Great Britain and Ireland* in 3 volumes; Vermont's *America Heraldica;* Crozier's *A Registry of American Families Entitled to Coats of Armor from the Earliest to the Present Time.* Clark's *Introduction to Heraldry* is often recommended to the student as is also Fox Davies' *Complete Guide to Heraldry*.

ENGLISH RECORDS

There are many sets of books treating of English records of various sorts. They embrace Court, Church, Parish and other records and lists, and are very good for consultation. They are so varied in the information which they impart that it is not advisable to list them, but to recommend to the genealogist when he reaches that part of his work where he has need of consulting books on English ancestry and origins to discuss the matter with the librarian where he is working and let him suggest the best books available in his library covering the matter.

MEMBERSHIP IN HISTORICAL AND GENEALOGICAL SOCIETIES

Before leaving the subject of books and their use in genealogical work something should be said regarding membership in Historical and Genealogical Societies. If the genealogist resides in a city whose public library has a good genealogical section he is fortunate, for he can then avail himself of the books, or at least some of them, for home use.

If, however, he is resident far from library facilities he will find it advisable to join some one or more of the historical and genealogical societies near his residence, or even across the country, from whose library he may be privileged to borrow books. So little can be accomplished by actual work in libraries, where usually the use of a typewriter is forbidden, that it is a decided advantage if books can be used at home where more and faster work may be accomplished.

Membership fees are not high in these societies, considering the advantages which are offered. The New England Historic Genealogical Society, offers the use of its library, one of the largest of the kind in the country, to its membership, and books may be borrowed by mail by payment of postage both ways which, under library privileges with the Post Office Department, is a small amount. This offers the facilities of this large library to any member, and though he may live in the most isolated section of the nation he is as near a first class library as he is to his mail box.

Not all books of course are open to borrowing privileges. Some are too valuable to be sent out and, in the case of reference books, the call for their use is too constant to allow their being taken from the library. But the number of borrowable books is great and the genealogist is wonderfully assisted by his membership privileges.

ORIGINAL SOURCES OF INFORMATION

Every searcher for family history will be tremendously impressed by the large number of families, some of them very prominent in American life, about which nothing of consequence has been gathered and published in historical form. Large genealogical libraries which raise high hopes in the mind of the prospective genealogist will contain on every shelf disappointments galore. He will discover that the continuation of his work will lead him to record offices in large cities where he will find well ordered files and indexes, and to small towns where there is little order in the arrangement of records; to cemeteries where he must dig among the grass roots for inscriptions grown indistinct with time, and to homes where old family Bibles once much used and showing wear and age will be brought down from the attic that their faded entries may be consulted.

In the published books he will many times secure great masses of material in a short time, but in unpublished records he will slow down to a snail's pace of progress in his construction. Many times this will be the test of the true genealogical mind. It is one thing to copy those items which are readily found and quite another thing to travel miles and spend days digging over old records and items almost unreadable to get one needed date of birth, death, or marriage.

ORIGINAL VITAL RECORDS

As has been said under the subject of "Published Vital Records," the obligatory keeping of such statistics by municipalities is of comparatively recent date. A letter to the Secretary of any state whose records it is necessary to examine will bring to the genealogist the needed information on this subject.

If it is found that the records as kept by town clerks and augmented by such records as could be gathered from the diaries of clergymen and physicians, from church and parish books, and from cemeteries have not been published, it will become the genealogist's duty to go to these various depositories and search the originals. It may become necessary in the case of published records to do this, as many errors appear in some of the printed books on vital statistics. In the author's own family name, the record of the children of Cornelius Stetson, of Westerly, Rhode Island, will be found in Mr. Arnold's work under the name of Austin instead of under Stetson where it belongs.

If original search is to be undertaken, arrangements should be made with the custodian of the records, otherwise a trip may be wasted. Some of the smaller town offices are open only certain days of the week or for only a short time each day. In many instances the records are kept in buildings and vaults where there is no heating arrangement and if the search is made in winter months the record books must be removed to some place where conditions will permit of the work being done. Unless previous arrangement is made, the genealogist may quite likely be told that the books he wishes to consult cannot be reached immediately and that he will have to come another day. This is discouraging information if he has traveled far for this particular task.

What was said under "Published Vital Records" regarding their completeness also applies to original search. Omissions and errors are abundant and there is nothing that can be done about it. In land and court records entries were usually correct, but in vital statistics and diaries they were entered without compulsion or supervision and they are exactly what the recorder chose to enter or omit. It was with him purely a private matter and he was answerable to no one but himself.

Nor is it unusual to find family differences creeping into the records as is evidenced by the following instance. On the occasion of looking up the heirs of a man who died several years ago there was found one living child, and the examiner was told that there was one son who died in infancy. The records showed the birth of a John and, soon after, the death of a Richard aged only a few weeks. Was John living? If so something was wrong with dates. Upon consultation with the mother, the examiner was told, "I wanted to name the baby John and his father wanted to name him Richard, but we named him John." It is interesting to read between the lines. Mother had her way, but Father got in the last word, even if it did complicate the records.

Thus vital statistics prior to obligatory recording, if not complete or in every instance correct, are very suggestive. Their record should be taken as good unless evidence to the contrary can be clearly established.

COURT AND LAND RECORDS

The indexes of Probate Courts and Land Records should be run for any help they may give. Wills usually recite the children of the testator by name and give the name of the surviving wife or husband. Administrations ordinarily recite the heirs at law and next of kin of the deceased. These are always helpful in furnishing information. Often will be found the names of other relatives, particularly if the deceased died without children.

Land records will furnish the given name of the wife or husband. When land is sold by a married person the husband or wife is obliged to sign off his curtesy or dower rights in order to convey good title. The discovery of an unfamiliar name will sometimes reveal a second marriage which had not been found from other sources.

The records of the Equity Court may also prove very helpful and should be examined if there is any hint of a division of property by the courts.

It should also be ascertained if there are early court records to be found. In the cases of early settlers these may prove useful. They are often deposited in the archives of some state department at the Capital of State House. They are available for examination and should be consulted for early history. Attention should also be given to early census reports, muster rolls, etc. as they are exceedingly helpful.

FAMILY BIBLES

The keeping of the record in the Family Bible was a universal custom in the early times, and of all available records is to have first preference as to its reliability. If a father and mother did not know such intimate matters as their birth dates, the date of their marriage, and the dates of the births, marriages and deaths of their children, there is no hope for the correctness of any other record. There is a record on the Clerk's books of a lower Rhode Island town that certain parents had a son Benjamin, born there July 9th 1772, but two family Bibles, kept by two of Benjamin's sons, give his birth as July 31st 1772. Without doubt these two sons who kept independent records knew from their father when he was born. They agree on the date, as they do on all other dates that are entered regarding the family. It is obvious that the Town Clerk could not enter a birth twenty-two days before its occurrence, but the doctor could have sent it in weeks after it occurred, or there may have been no physician in the case and the report was handed along by some neighbor woman, helpful at such times, so long after its occurrence that the definite date could not be fixed with certainty. Or the Town Clerk may have neglected to make the record until he was uncertain about the date. Or, the birth having taken place four miles from the center of the town and the record office, that was greater distance for news to travel in 1772 than ten times around the world would be today. At that early date the whole matter was probably passed along by word of mouth, and the wonder is, not that it was incorrect, but that it finally reached the records at all. Benjamin's was one of two births to be recorded in what was known to have been a large family of children.

The genealogist must consider all these matters and be charitable with a feeling of thankfulness that he finds as much as he does in the records, and he will consider the finding of an old family Bible as the discovery of gold.

CEMETERY RECORDS

In the minds of genealogists, gravestone records should have next place to the family Bible as to correctness, others place them after vital records in reliability. Stone engravers sometimes made mistakes which were allowed to remain uncorrected because of the cost involved in their correction. Sometimes mistakes were intentional as is evidenced by:

> *Underneath this pile of stones*
> *Lies all that's left of Sally Jones.*
> *Her name was Lord, it was not Jones,*
> *But Jones was used to rhyme with stones.*

And sometimes ambiguity was intended as is found on a stone in central Massachusetts, where is read:

> *I was somebody, who, is no business of yours.*

Incorrect dates on grave stones are not infrequently found. Sometimes the stone was not erected until long after the death occurred and until exact dates had become hazy in the mind of whoever gave the order for the cutting of the stone.

Gravestone records are very helpful for information in early times. The modern custom of giving only years, thus: 1830-1910 (which if the birth was in January of 1830 and the death in December of 1910, or if the birth was in December of 1830 and the death in January of 1910 gives a variation in age of about two years), was not in vogue in early times. The gravestone was usually explicit regarding dates, and often gave other valuable information. Sometimes the information was of questionable value, as on a stone in a northern New York cemetery where is recorded the name of the minister who preached the funeral sermon and the biblical reference to the text used. On a stone in an eastern Massachusetts cemetery is cut a niche in which is inserted a tintype photograph of the deceased over which is hung a marble cover so hinged as entirely to protect the picture.

Gravestones even become at times the medium of advertising as is shown by the following:

Here lies Jane Smith, wife of Thomas Smith, Marble cutter.
This monument was erected by her husband as a tribute to
her memory and a specimen of his handiwork.
Monuments of this style are two hundred and fifty dollars.

An examination of the stones in a family burial lot is strongly recommended. It not only may fix dates, but it may reveal members of the family whose record is nowhere else to be found.

Sources

In the *Benson Family Record* (published) is a list of the family of David and Jane (Seymour) Benson in which are the names and dates of ten children. These were found on the various records relating to the family. In the family burial lot, however, are stones for "Son David" and "Daughter Jane." In no other place are these children mentioned and were it not for a search of the cemetery there would be no knowledge of these two children who evidently died in infancy. They were a part of the family and should be included in any genealogy recording the children of their father and mother. By examination of the birth dates of the recorded ten children it will be found that between the fourth and fifth and between the eighth and ninth children as listed there was a much longer period than between any other births, and it was in those places probably that these two children came in the family.

INFORMATION SOUGHT FROM THE FAMILY

The amount of information to be derived from members of the family will depend entirely on the type of work being undertaken. If an Ancestral Chart or History is the aim, not as many people will be interested as would be if a Genealogy were in preparation. In the same proportion, not as many people will have information to furnish for an individual line as would have for all lines of a family. While the range of sources of information is governed by the class of work, the method of procedure to acquire the desired information does not greatly differ.

Whatever the nature of the work, the first thing to do is find the persons in the family who have knowledge to impart.

In an Ancestral History many different families are under consideration and so few individuals in any one of them have identical interest with the searcher that there is no great amount of work to be accomplished through family correspondence. In the *Handbook of American Genealogy*, a year-book published by the Institute of American Genealogy of Chicago, will be found an alphabetically arranged list under the caption of "Genealogies in Course of Construction." This list is keyed to another section of the book and will show who are known by the publishers to be interested in genealogies of certain family surnames. Correspondence with persons thus listed as interested in families of the surnames under consideration may prove helpful in securing information.

Because the busy genealogist should always, for the sake of labor and time saving, as well as for economy, use the printing press in place of his pen and typewriter where possible, a form letter is suggested to reach the persons found in this way. The letter should be printed on fairly thin paper because, as only one inquiry should appear on a sheet, several forms will sometimes be sent in one letter.

Carbon copies of this form letter should be taken, so that a record may be preserved and follow up letters sent out if necessary to secure a reply. In this, as in all inquiries, a self addressed and stamped envelope should be included with the letter. The letter may be phrased something like the following:

To...

....

....

Dear..............

    In preparing the records of the..................Family I am seeking information of the ancestors and descendants of the persons indicated below.

    I note that you are interested in families bearing the same surname. I shall appreciate any assistance you may be able to render or any suggestion as to a source of information which will help me in following out this line. I shall be glad to reciprocate with any matter which I may have in my files.

                Sincerely yours,

           ....

395 Everett St.,
Erie, Pa.

.........................*193*..

    This same form letter may be used for genealogical work to secure information of the families of daughters who have married into other surnames which appear in the index examined if it is desired to include them in a full genealogy.

    If a Genealogy is contemplated the task of securing information from the family takes on greatly increased proportion. There are a great many more people interested in the outcome of the work, therefore many more sources of information from connected families and individuals. Less can be gained from published sources of information and correspondingly more must be found from private and unprinted sources. The task, while approached in the same general way, is multiplied many fold.

The problem of finding and getting in touch with the various members of the family is an important one for the genealogist. There can be no real genealogy unless the members of the family are found and data secured about them. It must be realized that information is to be sought and found in every corner of the country, and that a small genealogy will index at least ten thousand names. That means data must be secured from a great many people concerning many individual families with which to build a genealogical structure. In this broad survey it is a most discouraging undertaking, but when separated into its various departments it is not so discouraging.

Like every constructive proposition it is progressive. The genealogist must be architect enough to see the completed edifice before the ground is broken, and builder enough to realize that the greatest structure is built by placing one stone upon another from the deepest foundation to pinnacle capstone.

The quest for information directed toward the family may well begin with a collection of Family Bible records. If there is a Bible stowed away somewhere wherein is written a record of a grandfather's family it should be taken out and copy made of its entries, and if there are other Bibles containing family records, in other branches of the family that are known to exist, they should all be hunted up and examined for additional items and variation.

With these items for a start the genealogist may visit the oldest members of the family who have retained good memories, if they are within his reach, and ask them as many questions as the traditional Philadelphia lawyer. These old memories should be started to working and encouraged to ramble on and tell all the history and tradition that they have stored in their years of intimacy with the family. These recollections should be carefully written out. They can be sifted and sorted later. All names and localities mentioned should be noted whether they are associated or not. The writer of a genealogy now in process of construction recently said that as a child he had a hazy remembrance of hearing his grandmother tell of cousins in a western New York town. No other member of the family remembered anything of them or their place of residence, but investigation found people of the same name in that town who had lost the line of where they belonged in the family. The grandmother's remark of many years ago seemed to be suggestive as a key to the whole situation. The names of these cousins were not remembered, but the name of the town, one word, was associated with the grandmother in memory and it is apparently enough to connect two large branches of the family.

Records should be made of the names of every person or place mentioned regardless of whether it is known at the time when and where they are going to be used, or whether or not they will ever be used.

There is perhaps no period in the development of the family from early settlements to the present generation which is so elusive as that age just prior to the memory of those living. Early history is pretty well known, and memory will reach back for three generations without trouble, but it is the intervening period that joins the early and the recent that seems to prove most troublesome.

The search within the family should also include any

manuscripts. Almost every family can produce one or more members who at some time have been ancestrally minded, and have attempted in a more or less perfunctory way to write their part of the family history. It may be that they have only made jottings of items, and never reached the writing out period. But the genealogist is usually told of an "Aunt Emma" or an "Uncle John" who once started to write the history of his immediate family. These histories may quite probably be found to consist of pencil notes on half a dozen odd-sized sheets of paper; rather a brief attempt to be called by the dignified name of a history, but valuable grist for the genealogist's mill. Several attempts may have been made by various members of the family all of which should be gathered and pieced together.

If there is a local historical or genealogical society it should be visited and its catalogues examined for any such fragmentary histories which may have been deposited there. Papers of this sort found after death which no one in the family cares to keep are often given to a local historical society where they are placed in an envelope, properly catalogued, and filed for reference. Sometimes such manuscripts are deposited by the person who has gathered the material and who realizes that it is too meager for publication and too valuable to be destroyed. Or it may be concluded that no one in the family has sufficient interest in the matter properly to care for the work and it is placed in safe keeping during the life, rather than left to chance after the death of its compiler.

There are many long and quite complete and valuable compilations that reach the historical society library in manuscript form because there were no available funds for publication. These are usually found in notebook form and sometimes represent years of painstaking work. Much valuable material may be found in this search.

In order to reach the large number of members of the family it will be necessary to make lists. Up to this point the genealogist, whether working on an Ancestral History or preparing a Genealogy has been working practically alone. In ancestral work he will continue to do so, but in genealogical projects the time has arrived when he must cease making independent examinations, copying his own findings and conducting the entire project as a lone worker. Help must be enlisted from all corners of the country which are full of living members of the family. From being a lone compiler he becomes an editor joining the work of others with his own compilation. It is essential that interest in the project should become family wide. Every living member of the name should be reached if the whole family bearing the surname is being covered, and every one of the living members of the lines to be carried down should be reached if the work is limited.

Telephone offices may be visited where will be found a collection of directories of different exchanges and cities. The offices of the various city and town directory publishers may also be visited where can be consulted a sizable library of directories reaching from Maine to California. All of these sources of information should be examined for lists of those of the name under consideration. The larger public libraries also have in their business section, files of telephone and city directories.

The genealogist should get in touch by correspondence with members of the family in widely separated areas and have them all cull from directories and mail in lists from their sections of the country.

A genealogist recently said that in making lists she ran the indices of every genealogy and town history in the library of the Rhode Island Historical Society for names of her family. This should be done in some good library having a genealogical department.

The building up of a mailing list will consume much time and be wearisome. It is preliminary drudgery, but it must be done. If some members of the family having leisure time can be persuaded to assist in this work their help should be enlisted. Slight errors any one may make are not vital, as this is not to be any part of the finished work.

These lists will furnish the names of a large number of people who will comprise for the most part the male lines of the family. The female lines will have to be secured from questionnaires sent out and from correspondence.

In sending out questionnaires it is advisable that with the return of the questionnaire, lists of all known members of the family with addresses be included. These replies can be checked against the mailing list already gathered.

THE QUESTIONNAIRE

Information is to be sought from many people in preparing the genealogy. Obviously, personal letters cannot be written to all the members of the family who have been found, and if they could, the result would prove very disappointing. A

. . . . Generation . . . . Family

(

)

son of. . . . . and . . . . (. . . . .) . . . .

was b. . . . . at . . . .

died. . . . . at . . . .

buried at. . . . . Cemetery

Resided . . . .

. . . .

. . . .

. . . .

. . . .

. . . .

. . . .

. . . .

. . . .

He married _____

on. . . . . at . . . .

dau. of. . . . . and . . . . (. . . . .). . . . .

She was b. at . . . .

and died . . . . at . . . .

buried at. . . . . Cemetery

. . . .

. . . .

. . . .

. . . .

. . . .

. . . .

(OVER)

Children of. . . . . .and. . . . .(. . . . .). . . . .

Names in full, date and place of birth, marriage, death, and to whom married

This record was compiled by. . . . .

of. . . . . .Date. . . . .

Sources of data. . . . .

. . . .

Verified by. . . . .

FAMILY	GENERATION	INDEX	NO.
			PAGE

REFERENCE AUTHORITY:

NAME

LINE OF DESCENT:

NOTES:

FATHER'S NAME

MOTHER'S NAME

BORN AT   ON

DIED AT   ON

MARRIED AT   ON

TO

FATHER'S NAME

MOTHER'S NAME

BORN AT   ON

DIED AT   ON

RESIDENCES AND REMOVALS:

OCCUPATION OR PROFESSION:

MILITARY SERVICE:

BIOGRAPHY:

DIRECTIONS: Use one of these blanks for EVERY marriage.
Use plain sheets bearing the same number as on this blank if necessary for additional biography.
Give the reference authority for your information.
Ask for more blanks if needed.
FILL OUT AS COMPLETELY AS POSSIBLE, SIGN AND RETURN PROMPTLY.

YOUR NAME AND ADDRESS:

			FAMILY NOTES:
CHILDREN OF	**AND**	( )	

(1) NAME			FAMILY NOTES:
BORN AT	ON		
DIED AT	ON		
MARRIED AT	ON		
To			
(2) NAME			
BORN AT	ON		
DIED AT	ON		
MARRIED AT	ON		
To			
(3) NAME			
BORN AT	ON		
DIED AT	ON		
MARRIED AT	ON		
To			
(4) NAME			
BORN AT	ON		
DIED AT	ON		
MARRIED AT	ON		
To			
(5) NAME			
BORN AT	ON		
DIED AT	ON		
MARRIED AT	ON		
To			
(G) NAME			
BORN AT	ON		
DIED AT	ON		
MARRIED AT	ON		
To			
(7) NAME			
BORN	ON		
DIED AT	ON		
MARRIED AT	ON		
To			
(8) NAME			
BORN AT	ON		
DIED AT	ON		
MARRIED AT	ON		
To			
(9) NAME			
BORN AT	ON		
DIED AT	ON		*Continue on another p*
MARRIED AT	ON		*necessary to list mo*
To			*children*

delightful correspondence would be established containing a minimum amount of needed information, and that small amount in such jumbled shape as to render it almost useless. To get definite answers, definite questions must be asked. But in asking the questions great care must be exercised not to make the questionnaire so formidable in appearance that it frightens or discourages the person receiving it. People are unduly shy of question blanks. Those persons who will write pages of letters will, when asked to write their name and the date of their birth in a particular place on a blank, hedge about doing it. Some bugbear seems to arise and persuade human beings that they should not answer definite questions.

Let the genealogist be assured at the very beginning of his work that no living person can devise a question blank that every one will understand, and that the finest arrangement that a supermind could construct will be twisted about in all sorts of shape by some persons and finally answered in such a manner as to be entirely unintelligible.

The questionnaire should be as simple, as clear, and as short as it is possible to make it. It should cover all the points sought but not contain an unnecessary word. If there are explanations and directions for answering the questions they should be so worded as to leave no room for misinterpretation of them, and the less wording on the blank the better.

Of the questionnaires on the preceding pages, the first has been devised by the New England Historic Genealogical Society and used with success for many years. It does, however, have the limitation of being usable only for the male lines as will be noted by the wording which only allows for "son of." It would serve a double purpose if it were so worded as to allow for sons and daughters, laid out in a form similar to the second questionnaire. When making up a questionnaire it is wise to allow plenty of room to answer all questions, and to provide clear instructions on the margins where they do not complicate the questions asked.

Most people have knowledge of at least two generations back of themselves and it would seem advisable to send the questionnaire in such form that information of three or possibly four generations could be gathered from each person responding. This will bring in much duplicate information which is not to be shunned as it fortifies the genealogist against errors. With this in mind let there be sent to each person four sheets, three of which should be the form shown above and one plain sheet bearing only the heading

The following are the names and addresses of other members of the family:

Assuming that the genealogist is to write the history of the descendants of William Curtis who came to New England in the "Lion" in 1632, with the questionnaire should go a letter printed something after the following order:

OFFICE OF THE GENEALOGIST

OF THE

CURTIS FAMILY IN AMERICA

. . . .

Dear Cousin:—
    It is purposed to gather and publish the genealogy of the descendants of William Curtis who came to New England in

the ship "Lion" in 1632 and was in Boston that year and later in Roxbury.

To assist in this work will you fill out the enclosed blanks and return them to this office as soon as possible.

There are four sheets enclosed.

The *first* sheet is for the use of yourself and your own family and should be headed by your own name.

The *second* sheet is for the family of your parent in the Curtis line and should be headed with that parent's name and the family carried out.

The *third* sheet is for the family of your grandparent on the Curtis side and should be headed with that grandparent's name and the family carried out.

Full names should be given in every case. Any information about which there is question should be indicated under "Notes" as marked on the blank that further investigation may be undertaken in connection with it, thus insuring correctness.

The *fourth* sheet is for sending in name and addresses of other persons known to be descendants of William Curtis.

Please give all the assistance you can.

Sincerely,

Address all communications to *Charles G. Curtis*
10 Main St., Jamesville, Mass.

The form pages should be identical and that they may be kept in proper order it is suggested that they be fastened at the top with a wire stitcher.

There will be better response if the papers bear a number. People are more careful about returning numbered papers than those unnumbered. The psychological effect is good. They should be numbered in sets, however, and not as individual pages, the space marked "page" serving that purpose. The fourth sheet, being no part of the record, should be removed from the set after its return and after the information contained on it has been checked and properly entered on the mailing list. It may then be discarded.

It will also be found helpful if the family has title to a coat of arms, to make use of it on correspondence paper and questionnaires. While heraldry is not recognized in America with its principles of democracy, still there are many people who have respect for such things, and there is no doubt that the judicious use of the old family coat of arms will awaken the interest of many people as nothing else would. It is a fair means of securing cooperation and assistance.

It will be found helpful if a register is kept of the numbers sent out. It may be made in a blank book ruled for the purpose, keeping the numbers in progressive order on the left hand margin of the page. This will help to check up on those who are dilatory in replying. Names should be crossed off as replies are received.

INFORMATION SOUGHT FROM PUBLIC OFFICIALS

The genealogist must not expect postmasters to furnish addresses. It is not allowable under the ruling of the Post Office Department. It is permissible to address a letter to the person sought, directing it to the post office where there is reason to believe he may receive his mail. The receiving post office will make delivery or complete the address and forward the letter if they have any information making such action possible. If the sender displays his return address on the envelope he will soon know if his letter reached the person for whom it was intended, as if it did not it will be returned to the sender.

Letters may also be sent to the postmaster with a note stating that the genealogist wishes to get in touch with a certain family whose name he mentions; that it is believed that some member of the family is served by that post office and asking that the letter be handed to any one known to be of the family sought. The postmaster will gladly render this service. It should be remembered to affix a stamp in this case even though it is to a blank envelope as otherwise it would be an attempt to use the mails without paying the proper postage for the privilege.

Public officials are, as a rule, very willing to do what they can to help in genealogical work, but it is not fair to them to ask for extended examinations without asking that a proper charge be made for the service. Clerks of towns and municipalities, registrars and court officials are busy people. If they were to spend the time to do all that seekers for information ask of them they would often have little time left for their regular work. A thoughtless genealogist will sometimes ask for an examination of records that would take days of a clerk's time with no suggestion of compensation, and then be surprised when his request is ignored or refused.

It is fair to ask if the name sought appears in the birth, marriage or death records or in the indexes of the land or probate records. In asking for this information every assistance should be given as to probable dates and any item that may help the clerk to answer the query with as little expenditure of time as possible. Nearly every official will gladly render this service without charge, but it is safe and courteous to include a dollar bill with the inquiry.

If the clerk finds the name sought, the genealogist should

go to the record office and make his own examination, or send some one living in the vicinity to do the work for him. In his inability to do either of these, he should write to the clerk and ask the probable cost of having some one in his office make the examination and having secured that information, if he concluded to have some one in the clerk's office do the work, he should forward his check with the request for the examination. This will avoid the question of financial responsibility and the clerk can readily make the proper refund if too much has been sent or render his bill for the additional work above the estimate given.

INFORMATION SOUGHT FROM LIBRARIANS AND CURATORS OF HISTORICAL AND GENEALOGICAL SOCIETIES

Many people assume that one of the duties of a Curator or Librarian of a Historical or Genealogical Society is to furnish genealogical information to all those seeking it and to give instruction to those who wish to enter upon the project of building up a Family History or a Genealogy.

Such work is no part of the curator's or librarian's duties. His business is to guard carefully the books and manuscripts entrusted to his care and to rent or lend them to such persons who, by membership or otherwise, are entitled to their use; to see that they are given good care and properly returned to their place in the library after having been used, and generally to have the oversight and care of the library. From the knowledge derived from his position he may be able to make valuable suggestions to patrons of the library, and a good librarian is always willing to accommodate by suggestions and advise in every possible way any one who appeals to him for assistance in finding material contained in his particular library providing it does not interfere with his regular duties. Such assistance, however, must not take him from his appointed tasks. He is in no sense a teacher at the disposal of the patrons of the library, and if he enters into the occupation of an examiner he does so on his own time and at his own initiative, and any one seeking his services in this manner must expect to compensate him at whatever rate of wages he may choose to place upon his work.

A quotation on this point from a little handbook put out by the genealogical department of the Public Library of the City of Los Angeles, Calif. will express the position of every librarian, not all of whom can afford to print a handbook.

The library does not compile genealogies. Every effort is made to assist patrons making use of the books and material in the Library, or to direct inquirers to outside sources of information. But the actual examination of records and taking of notes must be done by the compiler of the genealogy.

INFORMATION SOUGHT FROM QUERY DEPARTMENTS OF VARIOUS PUBLICATIONS

Several of the leading newspapers and nearly all of the genealogical societies which issue publications, maintain a department of questions and answers for the convenience of their readers. Thus a genealogical exchange is maintained. To ask questions through this department is somewhat of a shot in the dark and while many times it will fail of results, it does not infrequently bring the desired information.

The *Boston Evening Transcript* has maintained a genealogical section for many years which has been helpful to a large number of its readers. There is no charge for inserting questions or answers, the increase in the circulation of the paper being the only compensation. There are, however, certain definite rules which must be followed and any one wishing to avail himself of the service of that paper or any other having a like department should inform himself of the requirements that he may secure the best results with the least trouble to an agency which is rendering free service.

II
Ancestral Records

CHAPTER ONE : *INTRODUCTION*

THERE are a great many more people working on their ancestral histories than are working on genealogies. People everywhere are seeking illustrious personages with whom they have blood connection in direct line.

Ancestral research is more fascinating than genealogical examination, because in ancestral work the examiner is usually the pivotal beginning point. He is intimately connected with every person found in line, all lines focusing in himself, while in genealogical work, the examiner is only one person among thousands of others who lay claim to a common ancestor. Instead of being a direct descendant of every person under consideration, he may be a thirty-second cousin of many and perhaps then several times removed. The personal element is very much greater in ancestral work.

For those persons who have never attempted research of family lines, ancestry hunting is far easier than the work connected with the construction of a genealogy, and is to be recommended as an exceptionally good method to gain training along the line of genealogical research. In the preparing of a genealogy, because of the remoteness of the commencement date the problems to be encountered are near the beginning of the task, while in the construction of an ancestral chart or history the work is being prosecuted from recent date to that more remote, therefore the problems do not present themselves until the worker is fairly well into his task with some experience behind him and his plan of operation fairly well formulated.

One must possess some ability properly to start a genealogy, but it is a simple matter for any one to understand that he had two parents, four grandparents and eight great-grandparents every one of whom came from a family entirely independent of all the others, that every marriage of parentage merges two families of different blood lines, and that the children of every marriage, while partaking of the blood of both the father and the mother, are an entirely new family composed of a new merger of blood and personalities.

When eight great-grandparents are looked up and properly recorded it is only a step to sixteen great-great-grandparents who will represent sixteen separate and distinct families in no way connected other than that they share the privilege of having been the great-great-grandparents of the same great-great-grandchild.

These sixteen separate and distinct families will probably show several very different family characteristics, many of which have been transmitted in some degree and merged in the character of the common great-great-grandchild. There is scarcely a more interesting study than that of the blending of family characteristics. A family trait is seen to jump intervening generations to manifest itself strongly in a remote offspring. Thus ancestral research takes on a larger meaning than the purely historical and becomes to a marked degree a character study.

In every family there are bound to be found many characteristics revealing the noble and the strong, the true and the splendid in human thought and action. And while there may be something of the false and the ignoble, it is usually in negligible quantity. The experience of the professional examiner who was reported to have been paid a thousand dollars to examine an ancestry and then a couple of thousand more not to reveal the result of his investigation, may find its counterpart occasionally, but seldom.

The genealogist perhaps should be cautioned not to take too seriously reports of the sins and crimes of the forefathers. It will be borne in mind that the witches of Salem were very wicked people viewed in the light of their times while in this day they are looked back upon as martyrs tormented in innocence. The question arises who sinned most, the Quakers or those pious old church fathers who condemned them to banishment and suffering because they had moral stamina sufficient to enable them to stand by their belief in the face of punishment. Many a black court record of the old days is washed white in the light of today. It was a crime in early New England days for a man to kiss his own wife on the Sabbath day while bundling was not an uncommon practice among young people, and allowed with the sanction of their elders. No genealogist can long persue his occupation without discovering how quickly children followed marriages, too quickly for modern conventions, but without any apparent stigma being attached to the incident either at the time or thereafter. Families where early indiscretions occurred seemed to arise as quickly to prominence in the civil and religious life of the community as did those whose regularity was a matter of record.

The genealogist will very often be reminded of the words of the poet:

There is so much good in the worst of us
And so much bad in the best of us
That it does not behoove any of us
To talk about the rest of us.

In going back three hundred years in American ancestry the search is to cover the entire development of American life. There will be found many of those sterling people who have contributed to make America what it is today; men who have defended themselves, their loved ones and their homes by great sacrifice; women who have heroically and with great tribulation brought their families into the world; children who have come to maturity with few of the comforts of childhood that are known to the youth of today. Those persons are the progenitors of the present American people, the history of most of whom never has been written and whose remembrance will only live as their descendants keep the record in their own lives and writings.

Introduction

There are many and varied interesting incidents connected with nearly all lives which are worth recording, and as time goes on and generations are added, events that are common-place today will be of increasing interest.

It is advisable and intensely interesting to build up a history of ancestry. Some ancestors have excelled in one thing, some in another. Some have accomplished fame in the professions, some in trade, some in science. Some have defended their homes and loved ones from Indians, some have defended their country from tyranny, some have defended great principles for the sake of humanity. A few of these things may be of sufficient prominence to have been set down by the general historian, but the mass of them will be left unwritten only as they are preserved in family writings. They will not make a book for publication if put together in an Ancestral History because, unlike a Genealogy which ever works in a widening circle of interested people, this will work to a narrowing point of one person or one family of brothers and sisters for no one but full brothers and sisters could have exactly the same lines of ancestors. It is a great contribution of accumulated biographies, gathered a little here and a little there, and though various sections of it will be of interest to people in those particular blood lines, in its totality it will appeal to only a few. Such an ancestral history may go back many generations through peace and war; through the families of great men and into the lines of the leading powers of Europe.

It is a simple and easy thing to prepare an Ancestral History. Like the preparation of a genealogy, there must be system and uniformity in all this work. All work should be orderly with a certain place for certain items and dates and every one in its appointed place. The genealogist should never form the disorderly habit of having to search all over a page to find the date of a birth. Birth dates should always appear in the same place on the page and all other dates in their allotted space. Thus the reader can quickly find what he wants without excessive search. It is just as easy to be orderly as it is to be disorderly. It is purely a matter of habit.

It is recommended that letter size sheets (8½ x 11) of paper be used for this project. But whatever size is selected should be chosen with a thought of the binder to be used to hold the work. The Ancestral History will become a manuscript book. Unlike a genealogy where the manuscript becomes the printer's copy, the Ancestral History as prepared by the genealogist is in finished form. Therefore it is essential to choose all materials with a view to their permanency.

CHAPTER TWO: *CHARTS*

THE most common practice in ancestral work is to prepare a chart. To prepare one, however, is but to construct a skeleton, and while every structure must have its framework, its bones, some covering on the bones will add to the picture.

By all means make a chart. It is necessary.

There are a great number of chart forms on the market which can be purchased for about any price one wishes to pay. All have some points in favor of their use, and each in the opinion of its originator surpasses every other system. Some are simple and some are exceedingly complex. It would seem that a chart as simple and as flexible as possible should be recommended. It must be simple enough for the beginner, and comprehensive enough to meet all the requirements. It should not be so arranged as to pile up waste paper for lines not found, and yet elastic enough to allow for all lines when and if they are found. The simplest possible form that meets the requirements should be adopted. To the experienced worker a chart elaborately worked out may be clear and plain, but he must remember that his work may fall into the hands of the uninitiated and, to them, be as a Greek puzzle and worthless.

The chart illustrated, which seems to fill the need, is perhaps as simple in design as possible. It can be added to as occasion requires, and it can be replaced by separate sheets in case of accident or error without destroying an entire book of bound sheets or a very large sheet upon which there is a great amount of work.

A person begins with himself if it is to be his own ancestral lines which are being charted (or whoever is the common offspring who is to become the basic point of the chart), and fills in his own name on the middle line at the left side of the page. His father's name will be written in the space marked 2, and his mother's name in that space marked 3, with the proper data of birth, marriage, death and residence where they are indicated on the chart. His parental grandfather's name will be in the space marked 4, and the parental grandmother's name in the space marked 5, the maternal grandfather in space 6 and the maternal grandmother in space 7, thus carrying on until the right-hand margin of the sheet has been reached. The person in the direct line of the father, and of the same surname as the subject at the beginning in space 1, will occupy the top line on the right-hand side of the sheet, in the space marked 16, who will be the great-greatgrandfather of the person in space 1, or the father's father's father's father.

At the top of the page following the heading, Chart No. 1, will be marked on the first page showing that it is the beginning of the record. To continue the line which has been run to space 16, a second sheet will be used which will be headed:

Chart No. 2
Continuation of Chart No. 1

and on the center line corresponding to space 1 on the chart

82

(16) Father's father's father's father

(8) Father's father's
father

B
M
D
R

(17)

B   M

B   D

(4) Father's father

B
M
D
R

(18)

B   M

(9)

B
D

D   R

(19)

B   D

(2) Father's name

(10) Father's mother's
father

B
M
D
R

(20)

B   M

D   R

(21)

B   D

(5) Father's mother

B
D

(11) Father's mother's
mother

B
D

(22)

B   M

D   R

(23)

B   D

NCESTORS OF

(1) Own name

(12) Mother's father's
father

B
M
D
R

(24)

B   M

D   R

(25)

B   D

(6) Mother's father

B
M
D
R

(13) Mother's father's
mother

B
D

(26)

B   M

D   R

(27)

B   D

(3) Mother

(14) Mother's mother's
father

B
M
D
R

(28)

B   M

D   R

(29)

B   D

(7) Mother's mother

B
D

(15) Mother's mother's
mother

B
D

(30)

B   M

D   R

(31)

B   D

Born
-Married
Died
Resided

shown in the illustration, at the left side of the sheet, rewrite the name of the great-great-grandfather as it appeared in space 16. At the end of the line in space 16 on chart No. 1 should be written the chart number on which the line is continued, thus (2), to show that the line will be continued on chart No. 2.

It is not necessary that continuation charts should follow in the order in which the names appear on the right-hand side of the sheet. The great-great-grandfather whose name appears on line 28 can be continued on chart No. 2 as well as that ancestor whose name appears on line 16. Whichever line first reaches the right-hand side of the sheet and requires continuation should be carried to chart No. 2, the next line to need continuation, taking chart No. 3, and so on until all lines have been continued. The continuation reference numbers at the right hand of the last name on each line on the right-hand margin will indicate where in the work the reader is to look for the continuation of the line.

The same method is pursued from sheet to sheet so long as ancestors can be found to record. It will probably be found that lines will be lost in some branches before the right-hand margin of the first chart is reached, but space is provided for them when found, and such time as they are found will be sufficient time to allow for their continuation. By this method there is no mass of blank pages left for unfound lines. Sheets can be added when required, thus conserving cost and the bulkiness of the record which would otherwise occur. It is just as easy to continue a line on chart No. 30 as to do so on chart No. 2 if twenty-nine charts are used before some ancestral line is found to reach the right-hand margin of chart No. 1.

The Binder

It is not advisable to use ring binders. They do not hold the sheets firmly with the result that the holes soon tear out, and if patched with cloth which can be purchased and already punched and designed for the purpose, the capacity of the binder is only lessened to that degree. There are a number of stock binders having posts instead of rings, and with a mechanical arrangement that provides for compression of the sheets at the binding edge which holds them firmly in place. It is advised in starting the project to fill the binder to its minimum capacity that firm binding may be secured, even though a large portion of the sheets at first are blank.

A binder should be selected which can be opened for the insertion of new leaves at any place in the book without an undue amount of work in caring for the leaves of the two sections between the opening and the covers.

All binders and papers should be selected of the stock sizes. There is no point in having odd sizes which require special binders or filing arrangement. Only added cost will result.

The Paper

Strong paper should be used as it will be handled a great deal and must be selected to withstand many years of wear. It is well not to select too thick a paper stock as the book will be large if any considerable amount of work is done on it, and care should be exercised to choose a paper which will retain its color without fading or growing yellow or dingy. If a tinted paper, such as cream or primrose, is selected there is less likely to be noticeable any change than if pure white is used.

TYPING

It is strongly advised to have the finished work typed, even if someone has to be paid for doing it. Handwritten records never present the neat appearance and legibility of typed manuscript. It will be found advantageous many times while work is in progress on certain families if their record is handwritten, using one of the forms for a work sheet, but after all the data have been secured, the record should be typed and the work sheet discarded.

CHAPTER THREE : *FORMS*

A DEFINITE form is recommended for an Ancestral History. Thus uniformity can be assured and the record of every person included will be arranged like the record of every other person in the history and its appearance and usefulness will be greatly enhanced. This form can be printed, which is preferable, or typed as needed. If it is typed, great care should be exercised to keep to the same arrangement throughout the work. The temptation is, when the form is being typed as used, to omit those items for which it is known there is to be no need in connection with a particular individual, with the result that the whole sheet is shortened and the work is thrown out of its uniformity thus bringing the remaining items of the form in unusual places which will cause confusion. The printed form is always to be preferred because there can be no change in arrangement, and if any amount of work is to be done it will be found cheaper to pay the small additional cost of printing a form like that shown herewith than to take the time to type it and guard against any changes and omissions.

In an ancestral history each set of ancestors, comprising husband and wife, with their family and history, will form a complete unit of the work, comprising from one to as many pages as are needed for the entire story. If it is desired for any reason because of some prominence to record something of the lives of children who are not in direct line, and more room is necessary than the vital record, for which there is provision, this should be done on the parents' biographical sheet as this is their only point of contact with the history. There is no occasion to pick them up for later consideration. They are not ancestors, and while their history may be very interesting as uncles, aunts and cousins several times removed, as collateral relatives they have no independent place in an Ancestral History. The only ones having any special interest, which will be continued in a unit of their own, being those next in line of succession as ancestors. If it is desired to carry out the families of children other than direct ancestors it should be done in connection with their parents who are in direct line. There should be no provision for side lines and if forms are used in recording them the work should be done with a special color of ink to show that they are extraneous and the sheets bound in the unit of their father and mother and paged as a section of their number. This will set them apart as entirely foreign to the work in hand and no direct part of the ancestry.

In the biographical sheet there will be occasion to record more fully the history of the family than is done in a genealogy. In the latter only that matter should be recorded which is of general interest to the family as a whole or to some particular subdivision of it, while in the Ancestral History anything of intimate activity should be included which is of interest to the writer. It will be noted that the individual booklet of an ancestor and his immediate family may very easily cover a dozen or more pages and become

FAMILY	GEN.	INDEX	NO.
			PAGE

REFERENCE AUTHORITY

NAME

LINE OF ASCENT

FATHER'S NAME

MOTHER'S NAME

BORN AT   ON

DIED AT   ON

NOTES:

MARRIED AT   ON

TO

LINE OF ASCENT:

FATHER'S NAME

MOTHER'S NAME

BORN AT   ON

DIED AT   ON

RESIDENCE:

BURIAL PLACE

OCCUPATION:

BIOGRAPHY:

CHILDREN OF AND   (

FORM NO. 8-B (ANCESTRAL HISTORY) PUBLISHED BY STEPHEN DAYE PRESS, BRATTLEBORO, VT.

(1) NAME

BORN AT   ON

DIED AT   ON

MARRIED AT   ON

To

(2) NAME

BORN AT   ON

DIED AT   ON

MARRIED AT   ON

To

(3) NAME

BORN AT   ON

DIED AT   ON

MARRIED AT   ON

To

(4) NAME

BORN AT   ON

DIED AT   ON

MARRIED AT   ON

To

(5) NAME

BORN AT   ON

DIED AT   ON

MARRIED AT   ON

To

(6) NAME

BORN AT   ON

DIED AT   ON

MARRIED AT   ON

To

NOTES:

somewhat of a monograph or brochure, which will constitute one unit of the Ancestral History.

In the Genealogy the worker is preparing the history of one family for the benefit of the many descendants while in an Ancestral History he is preparing a cross section of many families for himself alone. In the former he is appealing to general family interest, while in the latter he is appealing only to his own fancy.

FAMILY

The Ancestral History has to do with a number of families with entirely different surnames. On the form recommended is shown, blocked off in the upper left-hand corner, a place to record the surnames of the husband and wife constituting the family with which the unit deals. This will aid materially when going through the papers following the strain of blood of any one of the several families making up the history. It is set off as no part of the history but merely as an aid in reference finding.

In this space should be written the surnames of both husband and wife, that of the husband being written above that of the wife, and always in the same order that there may be no question when referring to the sheet which is the male line and which the female.

GENERATION

The block indicated Gen. on the form may be used in either one of two ways.

To record the generation of the persons whose surnames appear as the husband and wife of the family recorded on the sheet and their respective remoteness from the entrance of the surname into the history. By this method an account may be kept of the number of generation of each surname which enters the ancestry. For instance John Gooding as an ancestor of Arthur Hawks who is preparing the Ancestral History for himself may be the third of that line of ancestry bearing the name of Gooding, the Gooding family having entered the Hawks ancestry in the person of Mary Gooding, the great-great-grandmother of Arthur Hawks. She was, however, only the grandmother of John Gooding, the subject of the sheet, and therefore he was in the third generation from the entrance of the name into the history and against his surname of Gooding should be written in this space 3, to indicate that fact. John Gooding's wife was Sarah Hawks, and as a Hawks she was in the sixth generation from the entrance of the name into the history, therefore, the figure 6 should be placed opposite her name in the space designated.

The objection to this use is that unless the history is being written following the order of the ancestry backward step by step through the generations it will become necessary to figure out in advance from the place of beginning what figures to use in the generation space. As for instance if it is found that there is a Gooding Genealogy and that the Gooding lines can be commenced perhaps twelve generations back in England. Unless it is planned to back up from generation to generation from the entrance of the Gooding family into the History, the worker should carefully list the names of the Gooding family to come into direct ancestry and then by counting he can determine the generation number to use against each name. It is always safer in abstracting to work back in regular order from one generation to that preceding it and not reverse the order of work. Nothing but confusion and the liability of mistakes will be the result of working lines forward rather than backward.

If the dividing line is disregarded the block may be used to record the generation of the entire family recorded on the sheet counting back from the starting person who is the first generation. By this use the figure 6 would be the only one used in the illustration above as John Gooding and his wife Sarah Hawks · were the sixth generation from Arthur Gooding who is 1.

There are advantages in both methods and they may be combined by placing the figures of the first method described above and below the dividing line and at their right, allowing the line to cross through the figure, that of the generation as described in the last method.

It should always be remembered in ancestral work that the counting of generations is the reverse from the method used in genealogical work. In the genealogy the first generation is the ancestor and in the ancestral history it is the person of the present time who is the pivotal point of beginning.

THE INDEXING NUMBER

In the block printed Index, on the blank should be inserted the number which is used to designate the subject of the sheet from every other ancestor who may be considered in the history. It will be found that a plan of geometrical progression is the only one which can be adopted and followed without encountering conflicting numbers. The subject of the Ancestral History is numbered 1-0, his father 2-0, his mother 2-1, his grandfather on his father's side 3-0, and that grandfather's wife 3-1 and so on. It will be discovered that the simple rule to follow is that the number of the father of each ancestor is double the number of the child of that ancestor. (The only exception being that 2 is not the double of 0, but beginning the doubling process back at 0, one generation more can be kept in the lower numbers.) And that the wife is always numbered the next consecutive figure above her husband; that male ancestors are always even numbers, and female ancestors always odd numbers. For example, a grandfather is numbered 3-0, and the great-grandfather in the same family line 4-0; that the wife of the grandfather is numbered 3-1, and that her father, who would also be a great-grandfather, would be numbered 4-2, and his wife 4-3. The father of 4-3 would be 5-6 and his wife, the mother of 4-3, 5-7, the father of 5-7 would be 6-14, the mother 6-15, etc.

The number preceding the dash indicates the number of the generation reckoning the person whose ancestry is being worked out as the 1st generation. Therefore, his father and mother would be the 2nd generation, his four grandparents of the 3rd generation, etc. If the subject of the examination is numbered 1 at the left of the dash, his parents will be 2-, his grandparents 3- and so on, as far as generations are recorded.

Disregarding further consideration of the generation figure at the left of the dash, we find that to determine the number at the right of the dash is purely a matter of geometrical progression.

In indexing it will be remembered that every form will be headed with the name of a male ancestor, therefore, the number will be a generation number followed by a dash and an even number, thus 3-4. But on the same sheet will be considered the wife of that ancestor who is also in ancestral line of the subject of the history in compilation. Her number, being the odd number next following the even number of her husband, should be inserted in parenthesis following the number of the male ancestor, thus 4-2 (4-3), 8-262 (8-263). Thus showing that the sheet is devoted to two ancestors one a male and the other his wife, a female, who are to be considered together as one family, and that the two numbers, the one following the other designate that family.

By this method of indexing large numbers will appear if many generations are recorded, but this cannot be avoided without duplication, because there are actually as many ancestors as the numbers indicate if they are all found.

Numbers are automatically skipped for any line of ancestors not found. There is no duplication of numbering and no lack if every ancestor in every line is eventually found. In practice, however, this great number of ancestors does not exist because of crossed lines. Unless these crossed lines were encountered to reduce the actual number of different individuals, the work would soon produce more people than ever lived upon the earth. It will be found for example, that the great-grandfather of one line was Samuel Noyes, and that the great-grandmother in another line was Eunice Noyes, the sister of Samuel. Therefore the father of Samuel and Eunice would be a double ancestor and would be entitled from that point back to two sets of numbering figures. When this happens the smaller of the index numbers should be retained and carried forward, and the larger number dropped with a notation saying that it has been merged with the smaller number and giving that number. The crossing or merging of ancestors may occur in different generations as for instance a great-grandfather and a great-great-grandmother may be brother and sister in different lines, but this need not change the manner of procedure in dropping out one of the numbers and carrying both lines on the other number. It will be well, however, if a skeleton chart is made carrying out the dropped line and filed with that line in order that future reference to generations may be made easier.

Because of this method of procedure thousands will be dropped out and never used, as not only the dropped numbers but all their multiples are cared for in the merger. What seems like millions of ancestors will really be only a fraction of that number.

Dropped numbers must under no condition be again used. To do so would seriously handicap computation of lines. The fact that they are dropped does not render them free for use again and if the practice is attempted only confusion and failure will result. All numbers are theoretically if not actually used. This rule must be ironclad and never be disregarded.

The advantages of this numbering plan are that the number preceding the dash (4-) always tells the generation as reckoned back from the person at the pivotal point of the research, and that the excessively large numbers following the dash that would result from beginning the examination by numbering the pivotal person whose ancestry is to be recorded 1 and proceeding by simple geometrical progression in the male lines and adding 1 in the female lines, may be avoided.

The plan is very easy to follow, and if adhered to will produce no complexity. It is suggested that in the higher numbers a space be left between each three figures (10-24354) if the work is being typed, or a comma inserted if the work is being done with pen and ink. It will be a help in reading the larger numbers.

NUMBER

In the upper right hand corner of the form will be found a box marked No. This space is left for any special plan of numbering the worker may wish to use, or for cross references, or for progressive numbering. Should there arise a need for a special numbering space, this will avoid placing a number at random on the sheet which would mar the appearance of the finished work. It may be used if the time ever comes when the examiner considers his work completed, for a consecutive paging of the book.

PAGE

Directly beneath the box indicated No. is another, indicated Page. Here should be inserted the page of the particular unit. If there is much biography and the record is to be carried over from sheet to sheet the pages should be in sequence.

NAME

Here should be written the name of the male ancestor of the family to which that particular form is dedicated and whose number it bears.

LINES OF ASCENT

In ancestral work the lines are always ascending because the beginning of the history is of recent date and ascends to a more remote time, while in genealogical work lines are always descending because the beginning is at a remote date and comes down to a more recent time.

On the form which is recommended there will be noted two spaces marked "Line of Ascent"; one for the male and one for the female ancestor who, being recorded together on the same blank as husband and wife represent one family in the ancestral history. Their union being by marriage and not by blood, they will have entirely different lines of ascent and come from families in no way related unless intermarriages have occurred.

The line of ascent of the husband should begin with his father and follow back only the male ancestors on his side bearing the family surname. The line of the wife should be recorded in exactly the same manner, beginning with her father and following only her family surname as far as it is known.

If the genealogist is backing up the line from child to father he will know only the name of the next immediate ancestor of the line and thus have only one name to enter, that of the father of the subject. He may proceed by examining his source of information and after making a list, entering the ancestral line, which will be a guide for his future work on that particular family, or he may omit filling in the line until he has reached the end of his present source of information and then going back fill in on the proper sheets the line as it is determined by his work.

The former of these methods is recommended as it renders unnecessary the going back over the sheets otherwise completed. It also is a safe guide for picking up the line as the worker progresses, as it guards against errors and omissions. For illustration, if the Noyes line is under examination beginning with Sarah Luella, the mother of the genealogist, by backing up the line in the Noyes Gencalogy the following list will appear:

> Sarah Luella
> Dr. Bradley
> Isaac
> Enoch
> John
> Samuel
> John
> Nicholas
> Rev. William

Then her Line of Ascent will read: *Dr. Bradley, Isaac, Enoch, John, Samuel, John, Nicholas, Rev. William.* And the examiner will know that he must find these ancestors in this order for his record. It will assist with the future work if the page is noted against the name on which the records of each of these ancestors commences in the Genealogy. The little time spent in this way looking up the order of the ancestry before the actual abstracting commences will prove well worth while.

If at some subsequent time and from some other source the line is discovered back of Rev. William it will be necessary that the additional names be inserted on the sheets which are on file covering the family.

DATA OF THE FAMILY

The items relating to the data of the family are so clearly indicated on the form as to need no further explanation. It is of course important to know the parentage of both husband and wife, the time and place of birth, death and their marriage. Attention is called, however, to the items of residence, burial place and occupation. These might all become a part of the biography but it will be found convenient to have them uniformly grouped for reference and as they are items which are needed in every examination it is well to have a place for them that they be not omitted.

It will be found especially illuminating to make a study of the occupational trends which have entered into the life of the individual around whom the history is built. Residences are necessary as indexes for original investigation to verify conflicting data as well as to secure material which has never reached print. And for the same reason it is well to know ancestral burial places. Tombstones may add materially to data sought or they may be valueless.

REFERENCE AUTHORITY

The student of ancestry and genealogy should always keep in mind that he is a collector, an editor and a recorder. In no sense is he setting forth anything new in theory or in fact. He is simply gathering and combining data. The arrangement of his material in its combinations and relationships may be different from any arrangement which has preceded it, but it contains nothing entirely new. It may contain items never before published but it can only contain facts as they have been lived in the history of individuals.

Therefore the compiler should fortify himself with the authority for his statements. His data may be from original public records; from printed histories and genealogies; from family Bibles; from old letters and private records, or from word of mouth secured from some member of the family. Whatever may be the source and wherever gathered, there should be clearly set down in some proper place the source of the information. Care should be exercised in this portion of the work as it is very important. Information will need to be rechecked at times and it is necessary to know where it was first secured. Contradictions will be encountered and it will be needful to follow out the sources of information in order to determine what should be the correct entry. If the information is from a printed genealogy the book and page should be noted thus: Noyes Gen. vol. 1, p. 264; if from a town history it should read: Hingham Hist. vol. I, p. 346, etc. And if the information is from a private source the name and address of the individual furnishing the data should be recorded, as Mrs. Mary Smith, 28 Main St., Williamstown, Mass. Cemetery records should name the particular cemetery as well as the town in which it is located as, North River Cem. Colrain, Mass. g.s.rec. If the cemetery is small this is sufficient and if it is large it will usually be wise to go to the cemetery office for the location of the graves sought, or in the absence of an office seek the information from the sexton of the burying ground. If the data are from a family Bible it should be noted whose family Bible it was and who has possession of it at the time of consultation, thus: Family Bible of John Blake in possession of Lucy (Blake) Jones, 32 Linden St., Baltimore, Md.

The genealogist will never regret the time spent in recording very carefully his references. Many hours of future time will be thereby saved and discussions referred to a source of information which will save many embarrassing situations.

Space is reserved on the left hand margin of the form for this purpose. If several sources have contributed to the knowledge set forth all should be noted and it is suggested that separate forms be used for each source of information, but if it is concluded not to do this, they should be keyed either by parenthetical numbers or by different colors of ink, matching the color used in the information with the reference authority.

NOTES

It will be found advantageous to have on the form a special place to note certain events or items which demand especial attention as for instance "Emigrant ancestor," "Double ancestors" in cases where cross lines are encountered, or "See No. ——" for cross references, etc. This is provided for on the left hand margin below the space for Reference Authority. It will be found a useful space in which to enter odd bits of information which otherwise would have to be buried in the biographical section.

The form with data of the immediate family entered thereon will present the following appearance:

FAMILY	GEN.	INDEX	NO.
Catlin	3 9	5-48 ;5-49)	
Baldwin	2		PAGE 1

REFERENCE AUTHORITY:

Family Record in possession of Herbert Catlin, 23 Main St., Springfield, Mass.

NOTES:

Original settler in Deerfield.

Both were killed in Indian War

NAME   John Catlin

LINE OF ASCENT   John,John

FATHER'S NAME	John Catlin			
MOTHER'S NAME	Isabella Ward			
BORN AT	Wethersfield,Conn.	ON	Jan.24,1643
DIED AT	Deerfield,Mass.	ON	1704
MARRIED AT	Wethersfield,Conn.	ON	Sept.23,1662
To	Mary Baldwin		

LINE OF ASCENT: Joseph

FATHER'S NAME	Joseph Baldwin		
MOTHER'S NAME	Elizabeth Smith		
BORN AT	Wethersfield,Conn.	ON	Mar.15,1644
DIED AT	Deerfield,Mass.	ON	Apr.2,1704
RESIDENCE:	Wethersfield,Conn.1662, Branford,Conn.1665.		
	Newark,N.J.,Deerfield,Mass.		
BURIAL PLACE	unknown		

OCCUPATION: He was a schoolmaster

BIOGRAPHY:

Published by Stephen Daye Press, Brattleboro, Vt.

103

CHILDREN

While there is only one child, the next in line, who is vitally connected with an ancestral history, it is always interesting to know and to record the entire family of the ancestors under consideration. These children are uncles and aunts in some degree of nearness and should be of sufficient interest to warrant being named in the history and the vital statistics of their lives recorded.

Therefore provision is made on the reverse side of the form for recording nine children with the information of birth, death and marriage. If more than nine children are found in one family it is a simple matter to head another form sheet with the same name and number, marking it as a continuation and paging it 2, and on the reverse continuing the list of children changing the numbers set against their names as the need demands.

In the list of children it will be found helpful if the one who is to be continued as an ancestor in line is written in red or underscored or in some other way clearly marked to distinguish that child from others in the family who are dropped at that point.

It will be noted that provision is made for this record of children on the reverse side of the sheet and following the beginning of the record of biography. If the biography is continued on succeeding sheets the question may arise in the mind of the student as to why it is broken by the insertion in its midst of the record of children.

As a history of ancestry the children, other than the one who becomes an ancestor next in line, have no direct bearing on the history and the insertion of the names and data is a side issue. It would not be necessary to record at this point the name of the one child carried forward as all of his history is recorded on his own sheet and the numbering plan will be sufficient to place him properly without being mentioned on his parents' sheet.

The biography, therefore, will read continuously from one sheet to the next and the story of the ancestors be unbroken by this extraneous matter of children which is inserted in such a manner that, while it is included in the record, it may be omitted in reading the continuous story of ancestry.

There is provision on the right hand margin for any memoranda regarding any one or more of these children. If more space is needed in recording their doings the story should be properly woven into the biography of their parents.

The form on the next page shows a family of children recorded as suggested.

BIOGRAPHY

It would indeed be a barren life which could be of long enough duration to place a person in an ancestral position without there having occurred many interesting events connected with the person. These events may not be of sufficient general interest to warrant their finding a place in any printed history or biography. Not every man who heard and obeyed the call to arms on the nineteenth of April 1775 could be named nor his experiences or exploits enumerated in the history of the doings of that memorable day. To the reader of history he was merely one of the unnamed soldiers of the American Revolution. But to all of his descendants

Published by Stephen Daye Press, Brattle

CHILDREN OF **Ebenezer** AND **Esther** (Catlin) **Smead**

	NAME	BORN AT	ON	DIED AT	ON	MARRIED AT	ON	To	FAMILY NOTES:

(1) NAME: Ebenezer Smead
BORN AT Deerfield,Mass. ON Dec.5,1695
DIED AT Deerfield,Mass. ON Dec.5,1695
MARRIED AT ON
To

FAMILY NOTES:

(2) NAME: Esther Smead
BORN AT Deerfield,Mass. ON Oct.18,1696
DIED AT ON
MARRIED AT ON Dec.4,1716
To Daniel Arms

Had 11 children
See Smead Gen.p.17

(3) NAME: Elizabeth Smead
BORN AT Deerfield,Mass. ON Dec.24,1698
DIED AT ON
MARRIED AT Greenfield,Mass. ON Apr.6,1720
To Joshua Wells

Had 14 children
See Smead Gen.p.18

(4) NAME: Thankful Smead
BORN AT Deerfield,Mass. ON Dec.23,1700
DIED AT ON
MARRIED AT Deerfield,Mass. ON Nov.6,1720
To Daniel Graves

Had 8 children
See Smead Gen.p.19

He was killed by the
Indians at Greenfield

(5) NAME: Ruth Smead
BORN AT Deerfield,Mass. ON Sept.5,1702
DIED AT ON
MARRIED AT Deerfield,Mass. ON May 4,1721
To Edward Martindale of Deerfield,Mass.

1 child

See Smead Gen.p.19

(6) NAME: EBENEZER SMEAD
BORN AT DEERFIELD,MASS. ON OCT.12,1704
DIED AT GREENFIELD,MASS. ON OCT.11,1783
MARRIED AT GREENFIELD,MASS. ON DEC.8,1726
To ABIGAIL BARNARD OF SALEM,MASS.

(7) NAME: Jonathan Smead
BORN AT Deerfield,Mass. ON Jan.19,1706/7
DIED AT Greenfield,Mass. ON Apr.29,1783
MARRIED AT ON
To Mehitable, daughter of John Nims

Resided in Greenfield,Mass
Had 11 children
See Smead Gen.p.20

(8) NAME:
BORN AT ON
DIED AT ON
MARRIED AT ON
To

(9) NAME:
BORN AT ON
DIED AT ON
MARRIED AT ON
To

his participation in the fight for liberty are infinitely more interesting than those of any other man who heard the call to arms on that notable day. To them this is a chapter in his life which demands as full a record as can be built up from every source of information.

And that is only one of the many interesting events which may very properly go to make up an ancestral history.

Provision is made at the bottom of the form for a brief biography and if there is need of more space a plain sheet may be used and the biography continued to as great length as the compiler desires to carry it and events of sufficient worth to be recorded can be found.

Educational   If the subject of the sketch has acquired learning in any of the institutions of higher education or has been trained in any of the professions, a synopsis of that accomplishment should be included in the biography with notation of any honors or degrees which have been conferred upon him.

Military   It is especially urged that all military connections be enumerated and all the details of service given as carefully as possible. This will be found of greatest value for future generations in determining their eligibility to the various patriotic and hereditary societies. In this way may be found a picture of the ancestor as taken from descriptions in the war records.

For example: "Enlisted in Capt. Brownley's company, Col. Cushings Reg't age 18, stature 5 ft. 9 in." (1778). Served again in 1779, "age 20, stature 5 ft. 10 in." Here is seen the boy who grew an inch between his dates of enlistments. Or this other boy from Stoughton, Mass., who enlisted June 14, 1779 "age 16, height 5 ft. 2 in., in complexion, ruddy, drummer." The next year he enlisted again and is described as "5 ft. 4 in. fifer." He had grown two inches during the year and was promoted from being a drummer to a fifer. This particular boy served four years and six different enlistments and a very good picture may be built up from the varying descriptions of the boy as found in the record.

What descendant would not hail with joy the record of this boy of sixteen years who grew up fighting for American liberty? It does not stretch the imagination very much to see the picture of this ruddy complexioned boy of five feet two inches growing up amid such strenuous surroundings, first a drummer boy, then a fifer then a soldier, adding a couple of inches a year to his stature in spite of the hardships. Such entries should have a place in the biography in fullest detail.

Especially interesting is the account of an ancestor who took part in that long and bloody war with the Indians. This struggle covering many years was broken up in American history by various separately named wars, but it was ever the struggle between the white man who was trying to gain a settlement in the new country and the stealthy Indian who had little of mercy in his make-up. As an illustration of the story of these times and the people living through them the student is referred to such histories as that of George Sheldon.

Surely every descendant of Jonathan Wells of Deerfield who writes an Ancestral History will want to take from Mr. Sheldon's books the story of Jonathan as he has quoted it from early records as follows: "I shall give an account of the remarkable providences of God towards Jonathan Wells, Esq then aged 16 years and 2 or 3 months who was in the action (at the Falls fight, May 19th). He was with 20 men yt were obliged to fight with the enemy to recover their horses; after he mounted his horse a little while, (being then in the rear of the company) he was fird at by three Indians who were very near him; one bullet passd so near him as to brush his hair another struck his horse behind a third struck his thigh in a place which before had been broken by a cart wheel & never set but the bones latp & so grew together so yt altho one end of it had been struck and the bone shattered by ye bullet yet the bone was not wholly lossd in ye place where it had knit. Upon receiving his wound he was in danger of falling from his horse, but cathcing hold of ye horses maine he recovered himself. The Indians perceiving they had wound'd him, ran up very near to him, but he kept ye Indians back by presenting his gun to ym once or twice, & got up to some of the company." The narrative goes on for two or three pages telling how he stopped to help another who was worse off than himself; how he was finally too faint to ride his horse; and to save the horse set him free while he lay down to die; of the stopping of bleeding and recovery of enough strength to walk with his gun for a cane; of his further experiences with Indians until finally he reached safety and rescue.

Jonathan Wells lived to raise a family and there can be nothing in the ancestral history of any of his descendants to excel in interest this narrative of his boyhood experiences with the Indians.

Business   All business connections which have proved in any way noteworthy should be briefly recounted and the business successes enumerated. Many of the older generations were connected with the industries which have made America great, such as the early shipbuilding, the New England iron industry, etc.

Political and Religious   These should be taken into account remembering that they were a vital part of the life of the earlier generations and that they were of much more consequence in early days than they are considered today. Participation on the great religious movements like the establishment of the Unitarian Church as a split from the old Congregational faith of the earlier generation; the question of slavery which divided the nation for a time, or that great question which preceded it and gave birth to the independence of the American people and the establishment of a national life separated from that of the mother country. These were movements politically and religiously which divided families and homes and the position taken by an ancestor regarding them is vital to his story and should have careful consideration by those who are recording the family history.

CHAPTER FOUR : *ITEMS*

IT is of the greatest interest to preserve any bit of record of family life. The migration of the various families connected by blood into new settlements of colonial times; the methods of transportation; the conditions of living; the experiences of pioneering; any and everything which reflects the life and character of those families who were ancestors should be carefully preserved in the record.

LEGAL DOCUMENTS

It is always illuminating to read the preambles of land transfers between father and children where "for the great love which I bear toward my son James etc." a father divides the ancestral lands among his children.

The preambles of wills where with life drawing to its close a forefather recites in the opening sentences of his will that simplest of religious belief in the following phrases: "Being of perfect memory and, through the blessing of God, though aged, yet in good health, and knowing assuredly that all men are mortall & yt young men may die suddenly, & yt old men must die, and how suddain my own time may be in these desolating times wherein ye enemie seeks the destruction of our New England. Being through Grace and the merrits of my Lord and Savior Jesus Christ in good hope of my eternal being in Happynesse; to whom I committ my soule, do hereby as followest settle my outward estate which God in mercy hath hitherunto lent me." And then in tenderest terms makes provision for wife and children naming them and with minute care dividing the worldly goods which God hath "lent" him. How much can be learned, not only of the size of the family and their names and many times the marriages of their children, but how much of the character of the testator shines out of those old wills. How interesting they are to the generations which follow.

All such items should be copied into the history for they reveal what sort of men they were who sired the present generation.

Inventories of estates have their story to add to the history in that from them can be seen the home life of the early days. In these inventories can be found a description of the furniture in the various rooms of the house, the "bedstead and cord," "the Trundle bed," the "chest of drawers," the "warming pan," the musket and the saddle which hung in the kitchen, the pewter porringers—how clearly can be seen the old house. There is also the description of the clothing of olden time, the foodstuff found in pantry and cellar—the corn meal, the salted pork and beef in their respective barrels, the tallow candles for light. The books they had, the conditions of labor and the tools and implements which functioned in the various occupations—the broad axe and the adz which bring to mind the great hewn timbers still to be seen in some of the old houses. The surroundings and conditions amid which the youth were reared and the aged approached the end of their days.

All these items are of great value in building the ancestral history. They are the flesh upon the skeleton of vital statistics which change the record from a recitation of bare statements to a story as fascinating as any that pen can write.

This will become the means by which the genealogist grows from the mere recorder of facts in statistical fashion to the editor and the storyteller. While he is never at liberty to let the story lead him astray from fact, he will have ample opportunity to exercise his talent of creative composition.

OLD LETTERS

Not infrequently may be found old letters which have escaped the destruction of time. Letters from soldiers in the civil war in which are recounted the experiences of those days; letters from members of the family who pioneered recounting the progress into new country, the building of the first home, the rearing of the family; letters telling of a death, describing a wedding; letters full of counsel from an old father or mother to a child who has gone into the wicked world away from the tender watchfulness of parentage; letters from a son or daughter to those back home reciting new experiences and new life amid conditions foreign to the old home life; letters that for one reason or another have been treasured and kept.

If they can be attached to blank sheets of biography paper without mutilation or concealing any of their contents, that should be the method of treating them. If that cannot be done they should be copied into the biography.

Sometimes present-day letters of reminiscence may be secured recounting incidents of childhood, or signal events of early family life may be secured from members of the family who have lived long amid kindred connections and who have memories worth contributing to the family history. All such letters are good grist for the ancestral history mill.

ILLUSTRATIONS

Not unlike any other story, the charm and the interest of the ancestral history are tremendously enhanced by the inclusion of illustrations judiciously selected and properly placed. Fortunate is the genealogist who is adept in the use of the camera and carries it with him on his ancestral pilgrimages using it freely as opportunity presents worth-while subjects.

It is not always easy to find photographs of people who lived in the earlier generations, and many times when they are found they cannot be incorporated into the history. The old style tintype may be discovered but it is hardly suitable for a book illustration. However it is not difficult to secure photographs of old houses which at some time have been ancestral residences. It may be possible to find old rooms which have not undergone very material changes since the time of a birth or death or a marriage in the family. Not only the house and room in which the family have lived but photographs of their last resting place may be included. These all form a valuable contribution to the history and serve to make real the story of the ancestors who spent their years and reared their families in the houses and rooms pic-

tured or who sleep peacefully under the gravestones photo-
graphed.

Coats of Arms

While heraldry and its accompanying coats of arms has no
real part in the make-up of American family standing as it is
now constituted, still it is a source of interest in ancestral
research to know who in the lines of the forefathers of the
various families connected by blood were honored with the
right in the old homeland to bear heraldry and to display
coats of arms.

The present generation is giving extensive consideration to
this subject and the work of search and artistic skill have
become an important branch of the genealogical profession.

In the compilation of a family history it will be found
interesting to have photostats at least of the various coats of
arms to which ancestors were entitled, and if the compiler
has artistic ability, or wishes to employ it, these various
coats of arms may be drawn showing the proper lines and
tinctures which represent the various colors. These will serve
as one means of illustrating the ancestral history.

Signatures

Signatures of ancestors may be found in the printed histories and genealogies consulted and if they are not found
there it will be possible sometimes to find them on old wills
and legal documents in court records and papers. These
when traced form good material for illustration.

Thus it will be seen that the compilation of an ancestral history may become an extensive and a fascinating project—one that will lead far into most interesting fields. As a branch of the professional genealogist's work it will not have as large a part as the more formal production of charts, but as an avocation for any person who wishes to delve into the intimate lives of his own forebears, there is nothing that can excel it.

CHAPTER FIVE : *SYSTEM*

LIKE every other book which bases its story on fact and deals with individual lives it is necessary that there should be an adequate index by which means the story of an ancestor may be easily found. This index may be very concise. A sheet should be allowed for each family name, and the entire index bound into the front or back of the book, as the genealogist prefers, in alphabetical order. On the sheet assigned to a particular family line should be entered the names and numbers of the persons entering as ancestors, for example:

Rogers, Mary 3-7
Joseph 4-14
Samuel 5-28

If it is desired to index the names of the children of ancestors, which is not at all necessary unless one wishes to keep account of them for some future use, the names of ancestors may be indexed as above in a left-hand column and the names of children in a right-hand column of the same sheet, picking up again for the next in the left-hand column the child who was an ancestor, thus

Rogers, Mary 3-7 Joseph 4-14
Samuel
Mary
Sarah
Joseph 4-14

If separate sheets are devoted to each family name there will be no difficulty encountered as additions are made to the line and new names are added from time to time. The list will be so short as to render unnecessary any alphabetical arrangement.

ORDER OF FILING

Either of two methods may be recommended for filing the finished work of the Ancestral History. If relatively few lines are worked out, the sheets may be filed numerically. If this method is followed the sheet of the individual whose ancestry is being examined, being numbered 1-0, will become the first page in the book, unless the index is put in the front of the book. Then will follow in order 2-0 and 2-1, the father and mother; 3-0 and 3-1, the father's father and mother; 3-2 and 3-3, the mother's father and mother, and so on to the end of the book and the highest number used. There will be many breaks in the progression. Later work will fill these gradually as ancestors and lines are found who will fit into these broken places in the chain. The book will grow from all points of breaks in numbers.

The only paging necessary is the unit pages of each ancestor where more than one sheet of paper has been used to complete either children, second marriages or biography. The numbers of the ancestors is the index, and will form all the paging necessary. Each generation will form a completed unit or section of the history.

If, however, the book is to contain many lines of ancestry and become a bulky history, it is better to file by family alphabetically, using a division sheet between the families which may also serve as an index of the book and a chart of the family. This method will enable the reader to find any given line in its entirety without jumping from section to section in the book.

In compiling the Ancestral History it will be found that all families excepting the one line carrying the same family name as that of the pivotal person whose ancestry is being worked out, will of necessity begin with a female name, the change of name and the introduction of a new family line coming by way of marriage, the dropping of the family name of the wife and the assuming of the family name of the husband. For example, Jeremiah Hall married Susan Green. Therefore, the Green line will begin with Susan who brought her family blood into the Hall family. This will be true with every line except that of the father of the subject whose ancestry is being recorded.

Therefore, in beginning the history of any family for its final form in the book, the first or parental information page of the husband's family should be copied for the beginning of the history of the wife's family, i.e.: To begin the Green line the parental page of Jeremiah Hall should be copied, showing the proper index numbers, names of Jeremiah's parents, his place and date of birth, death and marriage to Susan, the names of her parents and the place and date of her birth and death. Then under Biography should be written, For the children of Susan (Green) Hall see the record of her husband under Jeremiah Hall.

Then may follow in order the units covering Susan's parents, her grandparents, and thus as far back as the line is worked out.

While the history of Jeremiah Hall will be filed in its proper place under the H's, Susan's sheet will be the first of her family and will be filed in its order under the G's.

It will be found advantageous for future reference if the name of the wife, Susan in this instance, is typed in red, thus showing that it is the duplicate sheet beginning her family, and not the sheet properly belonging to her husband and his family which is filed in his family line.

THE DIVISION SHEET

In the method last described it is advisable to insert a sheet dividing each family. This is both index and chart of the family. It may be cut from ledger paper of a different color from the regular record sheets and should be ¼ inch wider for indexing purposes. On the outer edge should be typed the family name (Green) and on the sheet should be charted the family in order beginning with the ancestress who carried the relationship into that particular family name. The number of the generation and index should appear; the date of birth and death, and the person to whom married. This while not necessary to the record, will be found of great convenience for future reference. This division sheet should precede the family record and will appear when properly made out, in this order:

Green:

8-107 Susan		1714-1797
	m. Jeremiah Hall	
9-214 Richard		1666-1724
	m. Elizabeth Barton	
10-428 Thomas		1628-1717
	m. Mary Cushman	

WORKING PAPERS

The compiler of an Ancestral History will wish his finished work to be neat and clean; a record which may be handed down with pride to future generations. In order to accomplish this, some method must be employed for getting data from various sources, from which the final compilation may be made. Family records, public records, cemeteries, are some of the many and varied sources from which the searcher will draw material. To carry about into all these places of information what is to be the final draft of the history would only result in a soiled and sorry looking accumulation of papers.

Therefore it is necessary to have some form of working papers.

The form shown and described heretofore as recommended for the finished history may be used, but it has several serious disadvantages as a working sheet. It is too large and cumbersome for use out-of-doors and in cemeteries where the worker is at the mercy of wind and weather; it cannot be conveniently carried from place to place without folding unless the worker carried a brief case, and it will have to be carried about a great deal; it cannot be mailed, as is frequently necessary without folding, and it cannot be as conveniently filed for reference.

The form shown herewith is the same as that used for working sheets in the compilation of genealogical matter and fully described under that section in this work. It is admirably adapted for the collecting of data of family history. Under Index is written the generation number followed by a dash and the index number, as explained heretofore [4-12

FORM NO. 1

GENEALOGY WORK SHEET

FRONT SIDE

NO.	INDEX
NAME	
FATHER'S NAME	
MOTHER'S NAME	
BORN AT	ON
DIED AT	ON
MARRIED AT	ON
TO	
FATHER'S NAME	
MOTHER'S NAME	
BORN AT	ON
DIED AT	ON
RESIDENCE	
OCCUPATION	
BIOGRAPHY	

AUTHORITY

FORM NO. 1 (GENEALOGY WORK SHEET) PUBLISHED BY STEPHEN DAYE PRESS, BRATTLEBORO, VT.

CHILDREN

(1) NAME

    BORN AT   ON

    DIED AT   ON

    MARRIED AT   ON

    TO

(2) NAME

    BORN AT   ON

    DIED AT   ON

    MARRIED AT   ON

    TO

(3) NAME

    BORN AT   ON

    DIED AT   ON

    MARRIED AT   ON

    TO

(4) NAME

    BORN AT   ON

    DIED AT   ON

    MARRIED AT   ON

    TO

(5) NAME

    BORN AT   ON

    DIED AT   ON

    MARRIED AT   ON

    TO

(6) NAME

    BORN AT   ON

    DIED AT   ON

    MARRIED AT   ON

    TO

FORM NO. 1
GENEALOGY WORK SHEET
BACK SIDE

(4-13)]. The remainder of the form so closely resembles the arrangement of the larger form as to need no specific detailed description. The same rules of putting only one marriage on a sheet, and of carrying more than six children to a second sheet should be followed. It will be found useful in future reference to work already done if the name of the ancestor or ancestress in line among the children listed on the back of the sheet is either written in red or has its individual index number marked against the name in red. Thus the eye will catch the wanted name without reading the entire page, when it is needed for reference.

Great convenience also will be experienced if either a separate sheet, which is preferable, is used for information from each individual source, or different colors of pencils or ink are used. If the latter plan is employed, care should be taken to list at the bottom of the page under Authority the source of the information, and see that the information from that source is written in the body of the blank in the same color of pencil or ink.

Filing the Work Sheet

The work sheets will have to be constantly used and should be filed in such a manner that they may be readily accessible. They should also be filed in such a manner that they may be protected against soiling and wear if carried about in a hand bag or pocket. To accomplish this result it is advisable that each family line should be separately filed, using the heavy craft manilla envelope number 10 which will withstand much wear and tear and is stiff enough to keep the papers contained in it from being crumpled and rendered difficult to use. Only one family should be filed in an envelope, even though the same family name occurs more than once in the search. Thus ease may be attained in reference to work already done, and no more papers need be carried about than are actually needed for the family under examination.

It will be found useful if the face of the envelope shows not only the name of the family contained therein, but also a skeleton of the family worked out, and should resemble the division sheet already described under the subject of final filing of the finished work.

On the reverse side of the envelope may be shown listed at the top the names of books, records and persons consulted with reference to the family data contained in the envelope. It is by no means an uncommon happening for a searcher to forget what he has searched regarding a certain family, especially after weeks or perhaps months have elapsed and he has been busy on other lines and finally drifts back to lines long ago laid aside.

At the bottom of the back of the envelope it will be found useful if there is listed the names of places where the family has resided.

Briefly, it will be found advantageous to have on the outside of the cover of the papers contained therein, any information which will save opening the envelope and going through the contents.

The outside of the envelope would then somewhat resemble the following:

CUSHING

4–5 Mary Cushing   1819–1891
        m. William Alexander

5–10 Peleg   1792–1831
        m. Thankful Smith

6–20 Solomon   1762–1857
        m. Eunice Wilbur

7–40 George   1733–1819
        m. Martha Howe

8–80 Thomas   1708–
        m. Catherine Niles

9–160 John   1682–1732
        m. Elizabeth Holmes

10–320 John   1657–1752
        m. Sarah Gray

11–640 John
        m. Mary Rigby

12–1282 John
        m. Ann

Windham Co., Vt. Gazeteer
Stonington, Conn. Hist.
Bond's Watertown
Stonington, Conn. Town Rec.
Denison Cemetery, Stonington
Mrs. J. B. Smith Letter (Filed)

Halifax, Vt.
Stonington, Conn.
Watertown, Mass.

III

Genealogical Records

CHAPTER ONE : *INTRODUCTION*

IN this section of the treatise it is purposed to deal with the subject of preparing a genealogy. This is a much more ambitious undertaking than that of preparing an Ancestral History which has been heretofore discussed. It requires more training and more careful planning. It deals with many more people both subjectively and objectively; therefore it will be a much larger work and will necessitate a plan which may be expanded as the progress of the task demands. It is attempted with a view of possible publication and, therefore, must be prepared not alone for the eyes of the compiler and his immediate family but for a large family membership and a studious reading public.

In the first section of the book certain rules, requirements and suggestions which applied both to ancestral histories and genealogies were discussed. In this section those matters pertaining only to the preparation of the genealogy will be considered.

While the compiler of a genealogy is an historian, his province is not to deal with community and national events, but with the development of a family. The history of a nation records facts in their chronological order and sequence as they have occurred in national development, but for the causes and principles underlying such a history the lives of individuals and individual families who compose the people of a nation must be studied.

It is the work of a genealogist to present the history of a family as a component part of national life. The family record lays the foundation for the national history.

The preparation of a genealogy is both a pleasure and a task. The Hon. Marshall P. Wilder once said:

"It is a sacred duty to preserve the genealogy and history of families, but our busy population are so engrossed in the present cares, that few have had regard for the past, or solicitude for the future history of themselves or their families. But to those who have a respect for their ancestral name I know of no more agreeable duty than to place on record the history and incidents of their lives and their relatives, that they may be preserved to the latest generations. In nothing is Divine benevolence more fully illustrated than by those ties of friendship and Fraternal love which bind the family circle together. Next to training the spirit for eternal life, there can be no more noble employment than that of treasuring up and perpetuating the deeds, principles and virtues of a noble ancestry."

Introduction

The pursuit of genealogy may be either a vocation or an avocation; a pastime occupation or a business enterprise. Any bit of family history is well worth preserving. If it is a pastime occupation to gather a bit here and a bit there for pleasure, these bits should be put together so that they will be of the most worth, not merely to the gatherer, but to others who may have occasion to examine his work. While the pursuit of genealogical knowledge may be an avocation, it should be planned in such a manner and the plan so carefully executed that it will bear the evidences of a business.

While the gathering and recording of fragmentary bits of family history should not be discouraged, emphasis should be given to the added advantage of a more elaborate plan of operation with a carefully thought out scheme of action. If a work is to have value and usefulness it must be approached from somewhat of a scientific or professional angle, which is by no means a difficult task in genealogical construction.

The preparation of a family history or genealogy is a long and a serious undertaking and, if its compiler has not some aptitude for the work it can become very burdensome. If, however, the genealogist is interested in such matters, the burden is soon forgotten in the fascination which the work arouses. There is perhaps no more absorbing occupation than genealogical research. It is hard work nevertheless. The chase for family facts leads over wearisome ways, but it is intensely interesting, and the length of the way and the tediousness of the hunt should not deter the genealogist from following family lines up hill and down dell, for at the end of the search there is always something to repay the weariness. It is work which to be done at its best must have preparation, systematic planning, and careful execution of the plan. The worker must not lose sight of the fact that his occupation is not for pleasure alone, but that a far-reaching and valuable production is being undertaken which is going to be standard, and probably the only work on its specific subject for many years; that it will be examined by many people for various reasons, and that its value will depend entirely on how well he has done his work.

The work cannot be hurried. The genealogist should never be so anxious to see his efforts in print that he slights his task. It is the work of years to examine the history of a family in its many ramifications and properly record the results of the examination. If time does not permit the completion of the work as originally laid out, what is done should not be imperfect that the entire family may be dealt with. It is far better to leave half a genealogy well done than a whole genealogy poorly done.

The preparation of a genealogy is often attempted as a hobby. This method of approach to the task is perfectly proper if it is borne in mind that it is a hobby which is not self centered in its pursuer. Genealogies reach out their influence and affect the lives of a large number of people. While the compilation of the history may be the product of the genealogist, the material from which it is built is the most precious property of many other people. It is their names, their families, their characters, and as such, it must have respectful treatment and kindly consideration. It must not be made the toy of a hobby. Granting that the work is taken up as a hobby, it is too important to be pursued without a real business plan and purpose. It must have a very well-matured plan of action. When a man makes his hobby the printing of a book embracing in its contents the lives and actions of a large number of real people; a book which is to find its place on the shelves of libraries and there join the ranks of lasting knowledge and stand in neighborly contact with the records of the great achievements of mankind, then the hobbyist must pause and consider his purpose, how he is to accomplish it, and what the work is going to reflect when it is beyond his recall.

The genealogist must bear in mind that when he essays to prepare the record of a certain family he has precluded all others from that particular field. His book will find practically all the sale there is for a record of that particular family, and if his work is poorly done it probably will not be remedied by any other writer for at least several generations, by which time it will be too late to correct many of the errors he has made.

The author of a scientific book expects that his work is going to be out of date in a short time. He is prepared at all times to see the advent of another treatise which will supersede his own. He has placed one stone in the scientific structure and awaits the day when some one will place the next stone on top of his work. But the man who writes the history of a nation or of a family has a right to expect, if he has faithfully done his work, that his record is to stand undisputed and unchanged to the end of time.

It is the province of the historian of a family to set forth the high and noble character of that family so clearly that it will be an incentive to the coming generations to maintain the family standard and add to the honor and achievements of the generations that have lived. It is the duty of the genealogist to reflect the real life of the family that those of the present and the future generations may know from whence they came. Every family will have its spots of sordidness which must not be glossed over, nor should the genealogist engage in gallery play. There were a number of people who came to America in the Mayflower; many who fought the Indians; served their country in its wars, and accomplished greatness in various walks of life. It is not the business of the genealogist to attempt any monopoly of the virtues or greatness of American life. It is solely his business to record the progress of one family from early days to the present time. The record may not be far different from that of any other typical American family which has developed through a number of generations in this country. It is his business to set up a line of descent in such a manner that it may be true and be relied upon as an authority. It is his high calling to set forth the life of a family in such a way that it may be an inspiration to youth, a comfort to old age, and a faithful record for the perusal of the generations yet unborn.

CHAPTER TWO : *SCOPE*

H<small>AVING</small> laid down certain fundamental principles under-lying the whole proposition of preparing a genealogy, the next point to be settled is the determination of what is to be included in the attempt.

How far back into the history of the family shall the work extend? Is it intended to begin in America, or before coming to this country; to bring down one line of the family, or several lines, or all of the lines known that bear the surname; to bring down those of the surname only, which includes the male line and the unmarried females, dropping out the other female lines as they marry and take other surnames; or to carry along for a time the female lines, dropping them at a definite remoteness from their departure from the family surname?

All of these questions enter in and they should be definitely decided before beginning the work, otherwise complications may arise which will become a serious handicap.

What may be called the accepted plan is to begin with the common emigrant ancestor and go briefly and somewhat sketchily back over some generations of the family in their English or European surroundings, spending some little thought on the derivation of the family name and its variations, additions and subtractions, and including a brief sketch of the ancestral home, thus laying a respectable foundation for the family upon which to build the American genealogy. This all may occupy one chapter of the book to be written.

This chapter must be more or less traditional, with a faithful attempt at the truth. Dates are faulty and scarce due to the fact that the most complete and practically the only records available are those of the church and the probate court. It was of no consequence when a child was born, but his baptism was a matter for church record. Neither was it important when a man died, but the church made record of his funeral and burial, and the court took cognizance of his will when it came in for probate. The contents of the will, many times, was all the history that survived the memory of the family. In it there was usually mention of wife and children and sometimes of in-laws and grandchildren. This was not always true, nor was it always safe to assume that the entire immediate family had been catalogued in the will. The assumption that a wife predeceased her husband or that a child died before its father was usually based on the absence of the name from the will, which does not furnish anything like conclusive proof of the death of either wife or child.

It will readily be seen that any attempt to build up a complete genealogical line prior to the advent of the family into America is futile.

Most genealogists are satisfied to go back into England, or whatever other country mothered the family prior to their emigration to America, and briefly set down what is reasonably supposed to be the early history of the family. Others are not satisfied until they have proved, to their own satisfaction at least, the family line to Adam and Eve. After all, what is to be gained by trying to trace the ancestry of any one family back to the Garden of Eden pair? All families can lay claim to the same progenitors without further proof than the acceptance of the record in the first chapter of Genesis which states that all mankind and every family on earth had its origin with the same parents.

Inasmuch as the genealogist must hang strenuously to absolute facts, when a genealogy appears with a very elaborate account of the family back into the exceedingly dim past, the question is bound to arise in the mind of the reader as to whether the author has dreamed as much concerning the history of the family since its advent into America, as he did its history prior to that time. If so, his record is discounted at the very beginning, and his exhaustive research for early beginnings will militate against his entire work.

The real genealogy of the family should begin with the emigration of the family to America and the emigrant ancestor should be numbered as the first generation. The family should have its feet firmly planted in the old country if possible. The ancestral home; the date of departure for America; the name of the ship bringing the ancestor to this country; the place of embarkation and debarkation, and the place of settlement should all be noted. These having been found and recorded, the history of the development of that particular family in America may be commenced.

At this point tradition is quite likely to appear. Perhaps the most common snag is that there were three brothers who came here, one settling in Massachusetts, one in Connecticut and the other either in Rhode Island or New York. While it is true that brothers, brothers and sisters, and fathers and sons, came to the new land and settled, it is not safe to assume. in place of any known fact to the contrary, because we find families of the same name in various parts of the new country who were contemporary, that they were close relatives who settled in these various places.

If the family cannot be established before its advent into America, the genealogist should go back as far as he can for a beginning. His work can be numbered so that any generations found at any time in the search which antedate his beginning point can be put in their proper places without in any way upsetting the arrangement of his work. A start may be made at any determined point and can be worked both forward and backward so long as data can be found.

The work will be simpler if it is found that only one emigrant of the same surname came to America in the early days. One of the hardest tasks facing the genealogist is the separation of early families by the same surname. An instance is found in the *Barker Genealogy* where eight distinct families named Barker came to America, which are summarized thus:

There was James born in Essex County, Eng., in 1617 who came in 1634 and joined his sister Christiana who married Nicholas Easton and settled in Newport, Rhode Island. James was one of the petitioners for a tract of land which is now Westerly, R. I., and settled there.

Edward Barker was born about 1625, was said to have come from England in 1640, and was a well-known merchant in 1650 in New Haven, Conn.

Robert Barker and his brother John were among the early adventurers in Plymouth, Mass. They settled in what is now Pem-

broke, Mass. John moved into that part of Plymouth which was later set off as the town of Duxbury and in 1638 he moved to Marshfield, Mass.

Richard Parker, with his wife Joanna settled, and is the only citizen known to have been in Andover, Mass., in 1643.

James Barker and his wife Grace and their son Barzillai were, with his brother Thomas and wife Mary, among those twenty Puritan families who came from England under the leadership of Rev. Ezekiel Rogers, and who were described by him as "Godly men and the most of them of good estate." They arrived in Salem, Mass., in December of 1638. Thomas died without issue November 11, 1650.

In 1682 William Penn came to America on the ship Welcome and with him came his friend Samuel Barker who belonged to the society of Friends. On March 27th, 1685, a grant was made to William Penn of two hundred acres of land and purchased by Samuel Barker. It was located in what is now Newcastle County, Delaware.

While there were Barkers in Virginia as early as 1624, the first record found of James Barker is that he was born in England in 1726 and came to America soon after his marriage in 1751. There were other Barkers in Virginia which the genealogist has not connected with the above James.

It will be seen at once that to segregate these various families and not mix them in succeeding generations adds tremendously to the work of the genealogist.

If this condition prevails in the family under consideration, it will first be necessary to determine whether to attempt the larger work of recording all the families found or only one of them.

It will sometimes be found that all of the family in America have descended from one ancestor; that there is only record of one emigrant bearing the surname, or if others came they died without leaving issue. This very much simplifies the work of the family historian.

It must always be borne in mind that the pursuit of genealogical knowledge may be made as simple, or as complex as it is desired. One line can be followed from a common ancestor. If there were in the emigrant family seven children who grew to maturity and had families, all of those families can be picked up in the father and worked down, or the family of any one of the seven children may be run and the others left alone. If only one line is run well, it is a valuable contribution to history. Rather than to begin too discouraging a work, it is suggested that only one line be attempted at a time. With the recommended system of numbering, lines can be added sufficient to engage the most ambitious worker.

It is the usual practice to follow one common ancestor down. That being all that interests the subsequent generations of that ancestor, or the record of whom they will care to purchase. This seems the fairer way for the purchaser of the finished book. It is true that Dea. Gregory Stone and Dea. Simon Stone were brothers and both emigrated to America, but the descendants of Dea. Gregory are not especially interested in the family of Dea. Simon, and they should not be asked to purchase the history of both families to get the half that records their own branch of the Stone family in America. To print two separate and distinct histories, it was necessary to publish verbatim in both books the preliminary chapter having to deal with the Stone family prior to their coming to America, but even so, the author has shown good judgment in publishing separately the two families.

The other extreme may be found in the Barker Genealogy referred to above, where eight or more lines were combined in one large volume. There was no attempt by the compiler to join any of the various families except those of Robert and John, and they were both born before their emigration. The only string that ties together the various families reviewed is that of name. It is fair to ask how much the Barkers originating in Plymouth County, Mass., are interested in the Barkers of Delaware or Virginia. The cost of so large a volume must have prevented many from purchasing it and deprived them of the history of their own family. If the same material had been bound in a separate volume for each family of the name a far greater distribution would probably have been secured and perhaps a larger financial return.

These are matters to which the genealogist must give careful consideration.

DROPPED LINES

The next important point is to consider whether lines are to be carried along after the female members of the family have married and changed their surname.

The common practice is to drop female lines as soon as they have been properly established in the families of their husbands. If this plan is followed, the name of a daughter should be entered in its order with other children of the family, after which should follow the date of her birth and death, the date of her marriage, the name of the man to whom she was married, his parentage with the maiden name of his mother, the date of his birth and death, and the list of their children with the dates of their birth, thus:

> Mary J., born Mar. 4, 1834 at Boston; died June 21, 1895 at Chicago; married Sept. 6, 1856 at Boston, Robert M., son of John and Mary (Jones) Smith, born July 30, 1833 at Cambridge, Mass.; died Feb. 11, 1901 at Chicago, Ill.
> Children:
>> Robert J., born at Chicago, Ill., Oct. 21, 1859.
>> Lucy M., born Evanston, Ill., June 13, 1861.

The name of Mary J. is not carried any further in the work. She is now considered a Smith, and sufficient Smith information is given to enable any one interested in her to select her line in the Smith genealogy where she may be followed down with her particular family. However, she was still the daughter of her father and his blood still flowed in her veins. Her children have as much of the blood of her father in their veins as have those of her brothers whose names are carried along and their history written into the book. The unfortunate part of this practice is, that when the reader is referred to the Smith genealogy for further knowledge of this branch of the family, he is confronted with the fact that there is no Smith genealogy containing this branch of the family in existence, and that when Mary J. was dropped from the genealogy of her father's family, she was dropped out of all knowledge so far as any record goes. It will be found that there is not a genealogy for one in twenty of the lines that have to be dropped by this plan. The result is, that a large part of the family whose history is being written, remains still unrecorded after the family history is finished and published.

This plan is not a history of a family, but the history of those members of a family who have not lost the family surname by marriage. It is the difference between the history of a name, and that of the blood of a common ancestor.

The difference in the amount of work involved is tremendous. While the plan of carrying male lines of the name, and dropping female lines when the surname changes, has every thing in its favor from the point of view of labor involved, still there is aroused a feeling of sympathy for the daughters of a family who pay the penalty for being girls and getting married, by being dropped and forgotten in their family history, while the brave deeds and numerous posterity of their more fortunate brothers are spread on the record, a record that is as much the family of daughters as of sons.

Another point raised, is that of the record of issue and heirship. Perhaps the greatest real value of a genealogy is its legal aspect in tracing title to property. In this relation it may be the determining factor in the settlement of land titles involving the homes and property of an entire community. Many old country farms which descended to heirs years ago are now city plats on which are built hundreds of homes. A genealogy that can enumerate all the heirs of the old owner of one of these farms may well be worth its weight in gold in deciding the validity of the title of such ancestral land. Many a title searcher has been driven to distraction to find, when looking for the heirs of a long departed land owner, that the family genealogy carefully carried down the families of the sons, only to say that there were daughters who married and left families. Their offspring to the present generation are just as truly the heirs of the ancient land owner as are the offspring bearing the family name. The genealogy as a book of reference may prove its worth in many and varied way, which must be considered by the compiler.

It has been the practice of some genealogists to follow down favored female lines whose history would seem to lend glory to the family, and drop the less fortunate. This always seems like gallery play and a plan to be discouraged as lowering the dignity of the entire work. The matter of accomplishment is not necessarily the mark of superiority of intellect or ability, but may be, and often is, but a condition of circumstances and environment.

The genealogist should have a keen sense of fair play, and while he has to deal with the noble and the sordid; those who are inconspicuous and those who have risen high in the attention of the world, there is no place in his work for contumely or braggadocio.

The plan of carrying male lines, and dropping female lines as soon as they are established in the families of their husbands, or the plan of carrying all lines in so far as they can be found, the limit of search determining the stopping point, should be decided upon and followed consistently.

CHAPTER THREE : *GENERAL*

G ENEALOGY has many practical uses and its preparation must be approached with due regard for the important facts which are to be recorded. There may be speculation as to what the future holds in store as its contribution to the character of the individual and of the nation, but there is definite knowledge of what the past has contributed to both family and country.

A good genealogy is a treasure, and a poor one is often an abomination.

In entering upon so important an undertaking there are several points definitely to be determined at the very outset. The genealogist is going to delve into matters private and public; valuable and inconsequential. He is going to become a collector and an editor. He is to deal with human events in their most intimate character—the family life—and reveal them to the eyes of the world. These events will be intensely interesting to him, and the success of his work will depend upon his ability to portray faithfully these events, coupled with family vital records, in such a manner as to make them reliable sources of information, and interesting and profitable both to members of the family and others who have occasion to consult his work.

First, last and all the time he must strive to make his record accurate. Its usefulness depends almost entirely on this element. Genealogy is a statistical record, and as such should always be borne in mind by the writer. No one expects to read such a record as literature, but he does expect to consult it for facts, and that expectation must be met and satisfied by the faithful genealogist. This point cannot be too strongly emphasized. All statements must be true in a genealogy, or the reason given for the belief that they are true. A book of statistics of a family is no place to record guesses and suppositions, nor is it a place to evade indisputable facts. The utmost caution should be exercised to get and give correct dates and spellings. Though they may be pronounced alike, Smythe is never Smith or Smyth in the written record and the genealogist must enter exactly what he finds, with no variations. If he gets variations either in dates or spellings, he must enter his authority for each and put them all in the record that he is writing. Varying dates of a birth, marriage or death may be furnished by different members of the family, in which event every means should be exhausted to ascertain the correct date, but if this cannot be determined, all should be inserted and a reference entered against each, plainly showing the authority for inserting it.

Care must be exercised not to fix arbitrarily dates that are in question. It is a great temptation when an 8 which was obviously intended to be a 3 is found, to put it down as 3 and let it go at that, trusting that it is correct. This should never be done. If the error cannot be proved, it should be copied as it is found and a note put in for explanation. A marriage may sometimes be found recorded as 1848, while the death of one of the contracting parties is recorded as having occurred in 1846. The marriage was probably in 1843 or 1845, the figures 3, 5 and 8 being easily confused in writing. It is never safe to assume in such cases. Let the reader do the assuming. In a recent examination it was found that of a wife whose age, arrived at by subtracting the dates of birth and death, was only twenty-three years, had left nine children. Though these statments are obviously incorrect as to one or both dates, no attempt should be made to fix the date of either birth or death in the absence of good evidence.

References may be keyed and inserted at the bottom of the page or they may be inserted in the text, thus: (Scituate, Mass. VR) or (Jennie F. Smith, Daughter). Either method is correct and whichever is selected is only a matter of choice.

Whatever else is done, no pains should be spared to be exact, and the responsibility for variations placed on whoever furnished the information, for on this point will hinge the value of the genealogy.

LUCIDITY

The genealogist should write exactly what he means and write it in such phraseology that there may be no question of meaning. Ambiguity is a common fault of genealogists. This is often occasioned by the desire to shorten the record to save publication costs. In a splendidly written genealogy recently prepared by one of the best genealogists in the country, is to be found:

> "Mrs. Mary Porter Proctor, daughter of Charles and Rebecca Lincoln, widow of Samuel."

Who was she, and who were her parents? She may have been Mary Porter Lincoln, the daughter of Charles and Rebecca () Lincoln, or she may have been Mary Porter, the daughter of Charles and Rebecca (Lincoln) Porter. "Samuel" was evidently Samuel Proctor, who was her husband. This could be straightened out by referring to her anteceding generations, but the reader should not be required to run hither and yon from cover to cover to get straight what the writer could have stated in unmistakable language in the first place. This is discouraging to the reader and a genealogy is too complex reading to warrant adding unnecessarily to its complexity.

READABILITY

Genealogies are not prepared for general reading, but for reference. Therefore their object, rather than to create any literary style, is to bring out in orderly fashion the family data in such a manner that they may be readily found and definitely understood. But in the presentation of names and dates there may be a choice of style that makes one form more readable than another. An attempt should be made to phrase the record in as pleasing a style as possible, and having chosen a manner of phraseology, it should be adhered to throughout the entire work. It should not be written:

Thomas Southworth, born in Boston May 1, 1866

in one place, and

Thomas Southworth, born May 1, 1866 in Boston

in another place. The information imparted should be arranged so that the eye of the reader may not be unduly taxed finding what he seeks.

In the Work Sheet it is preferable that the name of the place precede the date, thus bringing the date at the margin of the page where it can be easily caught for such mental calculation as is necessary to detect errors or improbabilities. In the printed book it is advisable to reverse the order because by doing so a more solid perpendicular line is produced, one place of birth often sufficing for an entire family of differing dates of birth. Thus the date can be placed nearer the name than could be done if unused space were left for place of birth. This is, however, a minor matter, the main point being to stick to whichever method is selected.

The same is true in the insertion of biography. If the vital record of the individual family is prefaced by any biography in one instance, it should always be done that way. It should not be placed so that it precedes the family data in one instance and succeeds it in another. In this also it does not matter so much which method is used, as that it remain unchanged throughout the book.

BIOGRAPHY

A good genealogy will present some biography. It would be a waste of good opportunity and unfair to the real character of the family not to record deeds worthy of preserving which have been accomplished by various members of the family; successes which have arisen from business acumen; honors that have been bestowed because of mental achievements or otherwise. Often these bits of biography are well worth remembering and passing along to future generations, although not of sufficient worth to be placed in an independent biography or brochure.

Care should be exercised, however, in the insertion of

biography that it is true biography and worth recording. Where the sentence:

We are favored with no information as to the pursuits or character of these parents, but infer that they are commendable and that both are on the stage of active life in their native city

occurs with very little variation many times in a family history, and

"Believed to be worthy and reputable people"

is repeated on page after page, or

"We always understood him and his family to be of good repute"

is recorded literally hundreds of times in a volume of twelve hundred pages, it is not biography, and good paper and printers' ink are wasted. That is merely hearsay evidence of family history, and following court practice it should be debarred. No one is at all interested in inferences and suppositions in a book purported to contain only facts, and the reader can guess as well as the writer.

On the other hand, biography that is so important that it has been published under its own caption should not be much indulged in by the genealogist. A brief paragraph summing up the important items of the subject is sufficient. If the reader wishes more detailed information he should secure and read the published biography.

Military records, however, should be inserted in the family history, especially those pertaining to early military activities of the country. Records of our late wars can be easily consulted and only the briefest record need be used in the genealogy, but early records are fragmentary and anything found should be included and the reference given for the record. It should be especially noted whether early military information is taken from some public record or from family papers and private records.

Public Documents

The insertion of such early public documents as copies of deeds and wills is often valuable and always interesting. Many times family history can be read in them which is more apparent than the mere wording would indicate. When we read in a will:

> *I give and bequeath to my son Robert my Wearing Cloaths which with what I have formerly given him I judge convenient for him*

it might be taken to indicate that the father had been to some considerable expense on account of this son, and in a way disinherited him in the will; that the son was destitute and found his father's old clothes "convenient." But when it is found in the land records that this same father, when in his eighty-eighth year, before making his will, and only a short time before his death, gave this same son a valuable "river farm," using the words in the deed:

> *In consideration of the fondest love and fatherly affection that I bear to my well beloved son Robert, have given, granted etc.*

it is evident that instead of cutting off the son with a gift of old clothes, the father made sure that he had his part of the estate by giving it to him by deed during his life, rather than by will after death, and that "with what I have formerly given him" was not the expense of youthful peccadillos, but the "river farm." Thus the son is moved from being the one least considered as indicated by the will to become the favorite as indicated by the deed.

Again, when a will bequeaths five pounds to a sister-in-law if she shall purchase a black dress for mourning wear after the death of the testator, there is revealed a trait of character that is most interesting. Certainly in the mind of the testator he was worth the public mourning of the in-laws, and fearing that they might not coincide with that opinion he made sure of the matter by placing the bequest in his will.

Thus many times there can be read between the lines of these old wills and deeds the real character of the ancestors which display family history in more intimate phases than could be elsewhere found.

The insertion of copies of old documents merely because they are old is worthless in family history and should never be indulged in, but if they can reflect the mind and character of an ancestor, they are well worth using.

It is always well to give the place of residence of the particular branch of the family under consideration, and especially the last known address, and the addresses of any of the branch who are still living.

An examiner recently had need to get in touch with a list of heirs and, finding a new genealogy of the family, he thought himself fortunate and his problem solved until he discovered that in over a thousand pages of record brought down to within two years of date, there were scarcely any addresses of the thousands of living members of the family. This goes to prove that the point in the mind of the writer is not always the point sought by the reader.

It is well also to insert the business or profession of the subject. This is useful to those who may wish to compile an occupational index of the family, such as early ship builders, etc.

Domestic Irregularities

Probably in no family in America numbering from ten thousand to two hundred thousand members, which is fairly inclusive, can there be found entire regularity of family life. The question of these irregularities is one of the most delicate with which the genealogist has to deal. In a recently prepared family history it was discovered that five generations back, a boy was born into the family without any apparent father, the mother having neglected the formality of getting married. From this irregularity in five generations had sprung numerous progeny bearing the family surname of the mother which, with many marriages out of the name, were clearly the offspring of the common ancestor, the genealogy of whose family was being written. It was discovered that from this irregular birth had come many of the members most prominent in the family bearing its surname; that there were in the fruit of this irregularity a larger percentage of college graduates and of people who had accomplished worthwhile things in the world, than from any other line found in the entire family.

What was the genealogist's duty in this instance? Faithfulness to his work would not admit of dropping the family out as they were clearly a part of the history. Neither could a husband and father be manufactured for the occasion, and if the proper father were found, the surname of five generations could not be changed at this late date. There is in such instances but one thing to do, and that is to record the facts as found. The genealogist is not a dispenser of morals but of facts. It is not his province either to accuse or excuse but to stick to fact and record it when it is beyond question. But in all irregularities of family life he must be exceedingly careful to prove the facts before recording them, and then he should fortify himself by giving his authority, otherwise he may face the unpleasant duty of either recalling and reprinting his book or paying some one for wounded family pride.

Abbreviations

The subject of abbreviations is one which should receive careful consideration by the genealogist regarding both his reading and writing. In old records care must be exercised that b. is not used for baptism rather than for birth. Usually baptism is abbreviated bp., but not always, and while baptism usually followed soon after birth in the early times, it sometimes did not take place until mature life. Care must be used in reading modern genealogical works as publication costs have sometimes entered to such a degree that unusual abbreviations have been employed. Proper names are sometimes abbreviated to the extent of hopeless confusion. In a recent genealogy, where the writer is dead and the sources of his information destroyed, there appears Eliz. for both Eliza and Elizabeth; Jno. for both John and Jonathan, and Edw. for both Edward and Edwin, all of which are different names and not different form of the same name, and some for which the abbreviation is not correct. Such cutting corners may save a fraction of cost, but the loss of accuracy very much overbalances any saving that may be effected.

On the whole, it is better to write out in full, both in working papers and the finished copy for the printer, all proper names. It will save more than it will waste.

There are certain abbreviations that are safe to use and if used consistently cannot lead to confusion. In referring to published records the names of Town Histories need not be written in full. Instead of writing *Weymouth, Mass. History Volume 3, page 365*, it is sufficient to write *Weymouth III 365*. If, however, it is Weymouth vital records to which reference is being made, the abbreviation should be, Weymouth VR.

Following is a list of abbreviations which may safely be employed:

Vol.	volume
p. or pp.	page or pages
b.	born
m.	married
d.	died
bp.	baptized
VR. or vr.	vital records
Ch.R.	church records
G.S. or g.s.	gravestone record
FB	family Bible record
s.	son
dau.	daughter
w.	wife
wid.	widow
ae	age or aged
unm.	unmarried

sp.	sine prole (Latin) without issue
res.	resided or residence
RS	Revolutionary Soldier
CWV	Civil War Veteran
WWV	World War Veteran

WRITING DATES

There are two methods of writing dates, both of which are in common practice among genealogists. The New England Historic Genealogical Society uses, and prefers that its contributors use, the form of writing the day before the month, thus: *30 May 1764.* Equally common is the practice of writing the month before the day, thus: *May 30, 1764.* The latter arrangement seems more easily read as it is the form found in every day business and the ordinary reader is more accustomed to seeing it in that manner.

It is safer on working papers to use figures in writing dates than to abbreviate the names of the months. Thus, *3/23/-1928* rather than *Mar. 23, 1928.* In writing by hand it is easy to mistake Jun. for Jan. and vice versa. And not infrequently Mar. and May are confounded. If, however, months are figured instead of written, care, should be taken to determine at the beginning of the work the method of placing the month and day, otherwise *3/2/1860* may be read *Mar. 2, 1860* or *Feb. 3, 1860,* in which event the use of figures would lead to serious error.

In the compiler's own notes and work sheets he will be obliged to do much writing where conditions are very poor, as in cemeteries and while conversing with people where no writing table is at hand, in which instances the best handwriting is put to a severe test. The record thus taken may next be consulted many miles from where it was secured and it is important that it be so carefully written that its meaning is unmistakably clear. The figured date also occupies less room on the work sheet than the written date. The complete year should be written in the record, thus: *3/26/1840* rather than *3/26/40*, as the record is covering different centuries. While the general time may be determined as to century in most cases, there are times when it is necessary to have the full year written, and unless the habit of doing it is formed, there is danger of omitting it on needful occasions.

When the copy of the genealogy is prepared for the printer, however, it will be necessary to have it typewritten and dates should be written either in full or by proper abbreviation of the months. The comfort of the reader must be considered and it is surprising how many people are bothered if months are figured rather than written.

Dates should be arranged on working papers and in the finished copy with a view for ease of comparison. All dates should be placed in the same vertical position on the page. This rule should apply both to the working sheet and to the finished copy, and the compositor may be instructed to follow the same rule in setting the type for the book.

References

References and authority should be given for all data contained in the genealogy. If some member of a particular branch of the family has been kind enough to furnish information of his line, credit should be given him for his labor.

And if he has carelessly and inaccurately done his part of the work, the blame for the mistakes discovered should be placed on him rather than on the compiler. The genealogist must depend largely on information furnished him by others. He cannot go all over the country looking in every family Bible; examining the original record of every town and city, or verifying data that have been furnished by some one who should know the truth of the subject matter that he has furnished. There will be instances of conflicting data and information, and where dates are in question, that the genealogist will be obliged to go out and check up by examination, but a large part of his material will suggest no irregularities or improbabilities, and he will edit and arrange the furnished material without question. Where data are being gathered from all sorts of places and people, and furnished many times from the memory of some elderly person whose power of remembering has weakened with age, there are bound to be many mistakes. Tradition is bound to appear in place of fact. There was never a genealogy written that did not contain many errors. It does not matter how exacting the writer is, others are going to err in the material they give him, and if he inserts it in his work without reference he alone is the one who will be blamed for the mistake. It is surprising how roughshod people can be in riding over little insignificant errors in their family history.

If a line is furnished by some member of the family it is well to give the name and relationship of the informant to the head of the line, thus:

Data furnished by Susan Jones, Daughter.

If the material is found in some town history the reference

should be given as (Hanover, Mass. 246), and if there is variation all references should be given as

> Gideon Studley, born 1/1/1855 (Abington, Mass. 443); 12/31/1854 (Hanover, Mass. 390).

If the record is from a probate the record should read

> Thomas Robinson was the son of George and Sarah (Standish) Robinson (Plymouth Probates vol. 3, p. 78).

And if from a vital record the reference should be (Duxbury VR). Cost of printing should never preclude references.

FORMS

The use of a printed form is recommended for both working papers and the printers copy. It is cheaper in time and effort and safer in use than to write everything out either by hand or with a typewriter. There are certain questions common to every line and person that require definite answers, and if a form is used there is no danger of omitting to answer any of these necessary questions. The use of a form will present the answer to each question in a uniform position and much weariness will be avoided in working over the material.

MATERIALS

Good paper should be used in all of the work. Paper is not a large item of cost and the ease of working on good material more than compensates for any difference in price. So called, pencil paper should never be used. It is spongy and soft in texture, will easily blot, ink will run if used on it, and pencil will cut into it so deeply that fine writing and figuring will be indistinct. A dignified and valuable work is being undertaken and tools should be chosen accordingly. The genealogist has entered the ranks of the professions, therefore he should avoid the tools of the tradesman.

Especially should great care be used in the selection of correspondence material. If letters and questionnaires are sent out on cheap, poorly printed and unattractively arranged correspondence paper, the effect will be felt at once in the answers that come back or the lack of replies. Cheap materials will at once suggest that a cheap book is in preparation, and carelessness in first appearances will lead to the inference that carelessness will continue to appear throughout the entire enterprise. The genealogist must approach an innumerable number of people seeking from them help in his undertaking. They will be asked to do real work for which their only compensation will be thanks, and the wish to join in a laudable cause. Therefore he should make his approach that of a gentleman in dignified attire, and his reception will tend to be couched in the same manner. If he approaches like a tramp, regardless of his actual respectability, he will probably receive a tramp's reception.

In avoiding cheap materials it is not necessary that expensive material should be used. Good material may be inexpensive but not cheap.

It is recommended that pen and ink be used rather than pencil. The easy erasure of pencil is a distinct disadvantage with papers that must be carried about, shuffled together and continually worked over. If pencil is used it will be discovered some day that a hard won item is so smudged that it cannot safely be used and that the labor of securing it was labor in vain. On the whole a fountain pen will be found to be the best working tool unless a portable typewriter can be carried about, which surpasses every other means of making records.

STANDARDIZATION

It is recommended that all materials be chosen with a view to standards already in general use. Paper should be cut to fit regular sizes of loose leaf binders and cards to fit card cabinets in regular use. It is as easy to do this as to create a lot of mongrel sizes that cannot be fitted to anything standard. It will be found that paper stock can be cut to regular sizes without waste. The cost of material is not large and can be kept down to a minimum of expense if special sizes are avoided.

READING INDEX

The genealogical worker should keep an index of his reading. He will have to consult hundreds and perhaps thousands of books in the course of his work. Unless he has a record of the books that he has examined and the subject about which he has consulted them, he will soon find himself bringing from the library books that he has had before and from which he has previously abstracted the necessary data.

If he will head an index card with the name of the book, the name of the author and the year of publication, and enter on the card the name of the person about which he has consulted the book and the Progressive Number of the work sheet on which is recorded the result of his examination, he will save himself much unnecessary labor. These index cards should be filed alphabetically by the name of the book.

CHAPTER FOUR : *WORKING PAPERS*

THE genealogist must not hope to do his work so perfectly as he goes along that it will not have to be rewritten and worked over many times before it is finally ready for publication. It is necessary, therefore, to lay out his work so that it can be amplified in any place; changed about as to arrangement; new family lines added; and generally built up without upsetting the main plan or running into complications which will necessitate any decided change of scheme. There is perhaps no work that a man undertakes where so many loose ends must be left for completion as in the compilation of a genealogy. It is patchwork that must finally fit together into an orderly arrangement to make the picture of an American family in its entirety.

Much valuable time is often spent and lost in the preparation of genealogies by the writer discovering in the midst of his work that his plan is not flexible enough to meet his needs, resulting either in rewriting and rearranging the whole job on a more expansive plan, or carrying on with a made over arrangement which is very liable to produce mistakes and lead to confusion of lines that is troublesome. Years of work may be almost hopelessly mixed up, and the compiler of the genealogy completely discouraged, because he did not have a well thought out plan and adequate scheme of operations.

There are many plans of arrangement, all of them having some virtues to recommend them, and most of them lacking in some vital point. The plans to be explained herein are built up from what seem to be the best of all of those in general practice with such additions as are necessary to make the work easiest to accomplish and most successful in results.

Bearing in mind that any genealogy of size is going to embrace many thousands of people, it will be apparent that any attempt to keep them in mind without careful numbering and indexing is futile. Also it will soon become apparent that the genealogist is going to meet very confusing propositions relative to intermarriages which, while they may be so remote as to render the actual relationship almost nil, are still unions that will form cross lines for which provision must be made. In a recent examination it was found that all four of the grandparents of a certain member of a family were descendants in the same degree from a common ancestor, and although each grandparent came from a different line dividing prior to 1700, still there was the complication of numbering, indexing and cross indexing necessary to keep straight the various lines.

If several lines from a common ancestor are being combined in one book, there must be cross references. And if several lines are being prepared, each carrying one line from the common ancestor, there must be duplication of work that the member appearing in more than one line may be properly placed in correct order in each book. Through one line a person may fall in the sixth generation, while in another line he may be in the seventh generation, and unless the numbering and indexing are very carefully done the result is not going to be clearly set forth, and the entire work will be weakened to the extent that the reader will not easily understand the true relationship intended to be conveyed.

It seems necessary to have a plan of working papers with sufficient flexibility to record a family of a thousand individuals, or one with an unlimited number.

Working Papers should be clearly understandable, and a printed form is to be preferred. If one has a set of questions to answer there is less liability of leaving out an essential fact. A form with a definite place for births, marriages and deaths, and the chronological order of issue with such data as are necessary concerning them, should be strictly followed. The form should be simple, its meaning and arrangement clear to the ordinary person, and so made up that it can be used by the genealogist himself in his own office or wherever he may have occasion to work, or be sent out to others for their assistance in completing the answers to the questions printed thereon.

Working papers should be printed on small sheets. It is often necessary to make records while talking to some one out of doors or over the telephone, and much work will be done in cemeteries, where the use of large sheets is a nuisance.

In the following illustration is shown the form of a working sheet which is both convenient and clear.*

---

*Lefax, Philadelphia, Pa. Corp. 1910.

TR.MK. REG. U.S. PAT. OFF.

GENERATION...

Name...

Born at...............................On....................

    Son of..(father)

    And..(mother)

Married at...........................On....................

    To..

    Born at...........................On....................

    Daughter of................................(father)

    And..(mother)

Died...

            ....Children

....

(1) Name ....

    Born at.........................On....................

    Married at.......................On....................

      To...

    Died ....

....

(2) Name ....

    Born at.........................On....................

    Married at.......................On....................

      To...

    Died ....

....

This form has much to recommend it. It also has its limitations and faults. The printing on the form is so indented as to make the writing line very short. It is designed for use of the male lines only, whereas it is necessary to make provision for carrying female lines, as regardless of the decision of the limitation of the work to male lines there will be occasions where the female lines must be continued, and they all should be carried until they are definitely established in the families of their husbands at least. There is not continuity of the story. The birth, death and marriage should be closely associated on the form for ease of comparison. There is provision for but one death. It is as necessary to record the death of a husband or wife of a member in line as it is to know the date of their birth, for which provision is made on the blank. Much would be gained in the ease with which the blank is to be used if the arrangement were shifted about.

While it is possible to carry the form shown in the standard ring binder, to those persons who have had experience in writing on sheets held together by rings the advantage is offset by the bother of writing on sheets so fastened together. The rings are always in the way and the hand of the writer must rest on them which does not make for ease or good penmanship. Ring binders have a very valuable use in fastening together sheets of data which are to be consulted and which may need to be changed from time to time, such as price sheets etc. but as a notebook to be written in they do not commend themselves.

The illustrations on pages 122 and 123 show a form seeking the same information (which must appear in any form used) with the addition of such other questions as are necessary for the gathering of genealogical data and with the arrangement of the questions in a more logical way. The entire line can be used for writing; either male or female lines can be carried; the story is continuous, and room is provided for such biographical notes as the genealogist may wish to make in connection with the member, such as war record, college degrees etc.

The working sheet should be of a size which can be mailed without folding. It should be large enough to contain all the necessary data and small enough to be easily handled anywhere and it should be a size which will fit the standard envelope both for mailing and filing.

PROGRESSIVE NUMBERING

Every page of Working Papers should bear in the upper left hand corner a progressive number which can be stamped on with a hand numbering machine or numbered by the printer when making the forms. This number has several uses. It is necessary for various indexing purposes. There will be occasion to send to correspondents Working Sheets on which have been written partial data, asking that the form be completed and returned, in which case the fact that it is numbered will assist very much. Numbered sheets are thought to be a part of a general scheme which should not be broken, and experience has proved that many more replies will be received if the sheets are numbered than if they are sent out unnumbered.

This system of numbering has nothing to do with the finished work, and it is of no consequence whether members of the family are numbered in sequence or not. Let the order of the sheets follow the work from branch to branch and from family to family, the index will care for the desired result. If sheet No. 2758 is used for John Sylvester, recording thereon information secured regarding him from the Hanover Massachusetts History, and six months later when the genealogist is working in the larger numbers, more information is found from some other source relating to the same John Sylvester, the next unused sheet, which may be No. 4320, should be taken, upon which is entered the additional information. The index card for John Sylvester will care for the bringing together the information on these various sheets when it is wanted. It is well, however, to take time to cross reference as the work is going on, putting the sheet numbers in the reference line at the bottom of the sheet, but this is not absolutely essential.

The Work Sheet should never be taken out of the files for the recording of additional data thereon unless it is done with a different color of ink. Otherwise it can not be determined what information came from one source and what from another. If ink color is changed the reference and the information which correspond in color will be easily distinguished. On the whole it is easier and safer to put the information derived from one source only, on a sheet, using as many sheets as there are sources of information.

When the final compilation is to be made it may be found that there are several Work Sheets, widely separated by numbers, referring to the same person or head of a family.

In the following illustrations will be found a Work Sheet bearing information derived from two sources, the difference in type representing the different colors of ink.

NO.	INDEX
2758	abdbe

NAME
John Sylvester

FATHER'S NAME
James Sylvester

MOTHER'S NAME
Mary Thomas

BORN AT Hanover, Mass. **ON** 1/30/1810

DIED AT ABINGTON, MASS. **ON** 7/26/1872

MARRIED AT **ON**

TO Susan Josselyn

FATHER'S NAME
SAMUEL JOSSELYN

MOTHER'S NAME
HANNAH FULLER

BORN AT ABINGTON, MASS. **ON** 3/26/1812

DIED AT ABINGTON **ON** 9/19/1869

RESIDENCE
ABINGTON

OCCUPATION

BIOGRAPHY

AUTHORITY Hanover hist. p.392
ABINGTON HIST. P.400

It is preferable to put on one sheet only that information gleaned from one source. For example, the preceding Work Sheet contains information from both the *Hanover History* and the *Abington History*. A sheet for each source would be better. It will be found that the saving of time and bother will more than offset the difference in cost of material.

There will be occasion to use two other methods of designation in other places in the work, therefore it is important to fix in mind the term Progressive Numbering. Hereafter when the term is used in connection with Working Sheets it will have reference only to the number in the upper left hand corner of the Work Sheet.

Generation Index Lettering

In distinction from Progressive Numbering wherein one person or head of a family may be given several numbers, there must be a generation Index Lettering or Generation Index Numbering which is never used for any other person than that to which it is first assigned, and which, when used for that one particular person is always reserved for him without change. Just as there is a place for each person in a family and no one else can be substituted for that person, so there must be a designation for each person which is his very own and represents him wherever it is found.

This is a form of designation devised to render flexibility in the compilation of data, assigning to each person as found a letter or number which will not conflict with any other person's letter or number, and yet will leave the work open for the insertion of the record of newly found persons in the family that they may be put in their chronological order, though they may be found at widely diverging times.

This form of designation may be carried into the published work as was done in the Lincoln and the Waldo Genealogies, where Index Letters have been used, and in the Chapin Genealogy, where Index Figures are used, or it may be dropped when it has served its purpose, and the system suggested by the New England Historic Genealogical Society adopted in its place. It must be followed, however, until the work of compilation is completed and all lines are closed to additions.

The explanation of the system will show its flexibility and necessity.

In chapter 2 of Part 1, under the title of "Sources of Information" will be found a full description of Mr. Lincoln's plan of numbering by letters with its variation of figures as found in the Chapin genealogy.

The plan has its drawbacks when applied to the printed book as done in the Chapin and Lincoln genealogies because the average user of the books is not a genealogist and finds it some bother to accustom himself to the use of the plan. Librarians universally condemn the system because in their busy lives so much time is expended to explain the plan to their patrons before they can work with the books where it is found, with ease and comfort.

It is, however, the only system worth considering in preparatory work. By its use there is no danger of confusing numbers. There is ample room in the numbering scheme for recording as many families or as many children in a family as can possibly exist without having to resort to fractional numbers, changing from Arabic to Roman numerals or adopting letters to help care for subdivisions of families. The plan is more scientific because it enables the worker to jump back over several generations and pick up a common ancestor without being obliged to back up the line. For example, using the letters adefa bc and adefb ae as representing two persons in the work, it will be seen at once without looking up the intervening generations that the two persons came down the same line through abef or for four generations and that as three generations are different, i.e., c and e representing the individuals under consideration, their fathers b and a, and their grandfathers a and b, the fourth generation back or their great-grandfather was the same person and their point of union ancestrally.

With any other method it would be necessary to look up both fathers and both grandfathers and even then there would be no indication in the numbering whether the lines ever joined.

The plan when mastered, which is quickly and easily done, has great advantages over any other in so far as it applies to compilation.

If sufficiently used to acquaint the student who has occasion to use genealogies it would be superior for the printed book, but until its use becomes general enough to be well understood by the lay worker it will continue to be troublesome to those who encounter it in their work and a nuisance for librarians who are called upon to explain the plan to patrons of their libraries.

The third system of numbering to be used by the genealogist will only be necessary in preparing the printer's copy, and will be the last operation before the manuscript leaves the compiler's hands. It will then only be used if the system of the New England Historic Genealogical Society is adopted for the printed book. It will be discussed with the subject of preparing copy for the publication.

It will be necessary to work throughout the compilation of the material with Progressive Numbers and Index Letters and they will be referred to as such in further discussion.

Taking up the form of the Work Sheet again the space in the upper right-hand corner is designated "Index Letters" and on that line should be entered the Index Letters of the person whose name is to appear on the next line which is designated on the form "Name," thus:

NO.	INDEX
2958	aabeg a
NAME	
Abraham Josselyn	
FATHER'S NAME	

Showing that Abraham Josselyn is in the sixth generation and that he is the first child of aabag of the fifth generation.

The heading of the Work Sheet (Name), should bear the name of the person in line of blood, regardless of whether it is a male or a female. The business of the genealogist is with the blood and not with the in-law. This should be followed by the name of the father and the maiden name of the mother, thus:

NO.		INDEX
3641		acgdb ac

NAME
　　*John H. Jacobs

FATHER'S NAME
　　　Thomas Jacobs

MOTHER'S NAME
　　*Sarah Jackson

BORN AT　　　　　　　　ON

It is suggested that the name of the person under examination and the name of the parent who is of the blood be checked in some way. If the work is being typed the asterisk (*) can be used, and if the work is being done by hand checking may be done with a pen. It should be done in some distinctive way that will not be confused with any other marking that may be placed against the name. This checking is especially helpful when names other than the surname of the family, are being run as in the case of daughters whose lines are being continued out of the family surname. By reference to the above illustration it will be noted that this has been done, thus showing that the relationship to the family is through the line of the mother, the Jackson family, rather than through the Jacobs' line of the father.

The name of the husband or the wife, as the case may be, should be given in its proper place with the same information regarding parentage. No check mark can be used with the husband or wife unless they also are descended from the common ancestor under consideration, in which case it is wise in carrying the names of their children, to use two asterisks (**) or check marks in heading the Work Sheet of each of their children. Sometimes in old New England families all grandparents are descended from the same common ancestor in which case as many asterisks or check marks will be used as there are found lines of descent. This checking is very helpful in keeping straight intermarriages.

DATES AND PLACES

It is found most convenient to write the dates of birth and death in conjunction for easy mental calculation. Errors can thus easily be caught that would escape attention if the dates were separated by other matter. And for the same reason the date of marriage should follow those of birth and death. The date of marriage should never be placed between those of birth and death as it breaks the continuity of the story. The line carrying the item of marriage connects the history of the husband with that of the wife.

With the dates of birth, death and marriage should be recorded the name of the place where these events occurred. This is very important in checking for correctness. It will be useful also for those readers who wish to prove their lines for admission to patriotic societies. It is disappointing to pick up a genealogy and find that the desired ancestor was born, married and died on definitely known dates, but with no information where any of these important events took place, and with no suggestion where to address a communication to the proper authorities for certificates, which are so necessary in proving these matters.

In the event of conflicting dates, which are not at all uncommon in genealogical work, it is valuable to know where to go for the official record.

The same facts should be ascertained for the wife, or for the husband, as for the person in line, and for the same reasons. In searching ancestral lines, genealogies are very helpful and many times can furnish data of a grandfather or grandmother who, while they may be an in-law in the genealogy where their names appear, are in ancestral line of the examiner, and in the absence of a history of their own particular family, could in no other way be found.

It is always advisable to furnish residence if possible. In the case of generations that are dead, residence often gives clues for other family data and possible descendants. For generations still alive, residence is very valuable to examiners working on other family genealogies where marriages have occurred with the family whose history has been published. In a very complete genealogy recently printed, otherwise very carefully prepared, this important detail is missing and the examiner having occasion to use the book in search of living members of his own family whose names appeared in the volume through marriage, found several hundred names of the people with whom he wished to communicate, but almost no addresses by which he could get in touch with them. Thus for his purpose the book was practically worthless.

It is also recommended that professions and occupations be included where they are known, and space is provided on the form for the recording of such information. Such knowledge will have many uses in the minds of the readers.

Room is also provided for biography. It is important to make note of any war record; of the educational attainments; and the noteworthy events in the life of the individual. In the large majority of instances the space provided is sufficient, but where more room is needed it is a simple matter to use a blank sheet cut the same size as the form which should bear the same Progressive Number and Index Letters and be treated as a continuation of the biographical sketch on the form.

REFERENCES

There should be in a place apart from the family data contained thereon, a place for reference to the books or people consulted regarding the subject matter on the sheet. The genealogist should very carefully fortify himself with the evidences of his knowledge or belief. It will also be necessary to know where to re-examine in order to check back if for any reason the record is ever in question.

In the form shown, the bottom of the page is reserved and boxed off for reference authority wherein can be written the name of the book and the page consulted, or the name and address of the person furnishing the information, thus:

AUTHORITY   Mrs. Ella J. Holmes
        (Daughter)   Racine,Wis.

or

AUTHORITY

        Weymouth,Mass III,p.253

With the completion of the history of the husband and wife the Work Sheet will be as illustrated:

NO. 2958	INDEX acgbd ac

NAME
    *John H. Jacobs

FATHER'S NAME
    Thomas Jacobs

MOTHER S NAME
    *Sarah Jackson

BORN AT Hanover,Mass.   **ON** 3/5/1850

DIED AT Rockland,Mass.   **ON** 7/24/1926

MARRIED AT Hanover,Mass.   **ON** 1/1/1872

TO
    Mary R. Sampson

FATHER'S NAME
    William Sampson

MOTHER'S NAME
    Mary Russell

BORN AT Abington,Mass.   **ON** 7/2/1852

DIED AT Rockland,Mass.   **ON** 9/18/1897

RESIDENCE
    Rockland,Mass.

OCCUPATION
    Farmer and carpenter

BIOGRAPHY
    Representative Mass. Legislature

    1878-9

    Selectman 1880-1886

RECORDING CHILDREN

In the form illustrated provision is made for six children. The size of the form can accommodate that number with the proper data concerning each, and six is usually a sufficient number for which to provide. In larger families it is easier and cheaper to use a second or even a third sheet, changing the index letters or numbers opposite the names of the children as needful. In using additional sheets in this way succeeding Progressive Numbers should be used, but retaining the same Generation Index Letters or Numbers.

While it was a common occurrence to find families of ten or more children one hundred years ago, thus requiring two Work Sheets for their recording, the average family for the last fifty years will record less than six children. It will be found that there is ample provision on the blank for a large percentage of the families with which the genealogist has to deal, and that provision for larger families would be paper wasted and added bulk in handling and filing.

Data regarding children should contain for each child the name, place and date of birth, death and marriage, and to whom married. Also residence should be recorded. If there is no issue of the union, there is no need for further record, but if there is issue, a new sheet should be started bearing the name of that child, the proper Index Letters, and at the bottom of the sheet in the Authority box the Progressive Number of the parent from whose Work Sheet the record has been transferred. The Progressive Number of the child's Work Sheet should also be marked against his name on the parent's Work Sheet, thus cross referencing and tying together the records of parent and child for convenience in later work.

The Work Sheet of a parent with a first child who married and died without issue; of a second child who married and had issue; and of a third child who died unmarried is shown in the illustration below. It will be noted that the record of the first and third child are ended on the Work Sheet of the parent, but that of the second child is transferred to an independent Work Sheet of his own for continuation.

3 CHILDREN		
(1) NAME Grace M. Jacobs		
BORN AT Rockland, Mass.	**ON** 9/26/1873	
DIED AT Rockland	**ON** 7/6/1897	
MARRIED AT Rockland	**ON** 2/5/1894	
TO George R. Hill	sp	

(2) NAME George J. Jacobs		
BORN AT Rockland	**ON** 10/3/1875	
DIED AT (2975)	**ON**	
MARRIED AT	**ON**	
TO		

(3) NAME Mary M. Jacobs		
BORN AT Rockland	**ON** 4/7/1878	
DIED AT Rockland	**ON** 9/6/1878	
MARRIED AT	**ON**	
TO		

NO.	INDEX
2972	acgbd acb.

NAME
*George J. Jacobs

FATHER'S NAME
*John H. Jacobs

MOTHER'S NAME
Mary R. Sampson

BORN AT   **ON**
Rockland, Mass.   10/3/1875

DIED AT   **ON**

MARRIED AT   **ON**

TO

FATHER'S NAME

MOTHER'S NAME

BORN AT   **ON**

DIED AT   **ON**

RESIDENCE

OCCUPATION

BIOGRAPHY

AUTHORITY
Hanover p.347

SUCCESSIVE MARRIAGES

In the event that the subject of the Work Sheet has married more than once a separate Work Sheet should be used for each marriage, and the children of each union should be recorded on the Work Sheet of their parents.

In heading the second marriage Work Sheet it is not necessary to repeat the data of the subject of the sheet, but the Generation Index Letters and the name should be repeated.

Had John H. Jacobs married a second time his Work Sheet would be headed as follows:

NO.	INDEX
2959	acgdb ac Con.

NAME	* John H. Jacobs
FATHER'S NAME	
MOTHER S NAME	
BORN AT	ON
DIED AT	ON
MARRIED AT	2nd. Rockland, Mass. ON 2/2/1898
TO	Mary Smith
FATHER'S NAME	John Smith
MOTHER'S NAME	Sarah Jones
BORN AT	Abington, Mass. ON 7/3/1858
DIED AT	Rockland, Mass. ON 10/3/1927
RESIDENCE	
OCCUPATION	
BIOGRAPHY	

FIELD WORKING PAPERS

The same form may be used for what may be called Field Working Papers, i.e. for gathering information from others, principally by correspondence. While it will not take the place of the Questionnaire already described, for the securing of entirely new data, it will be found better than the other form for the completion of partial data.

The seeker after information is always handicapped when he has to resort to the mails. Many people are totally uninterested in family history. Others are woefully ignorant of their family data. Some do not realize how little they really do know about their family affairs as was recently illustrated by the experience of a title examiner seeking the heirs of a dead land owner. A certain member of the family told the examiner that he knew the complete history of the family and could furnish all that was needed in the case. When it came to definite information, however, he could not name, without the aid of his wife, the date of birth of any of his own children or tell how old they were, nor did he know the names of all of his grandfather's children, his own uncles and aunts.

This lack of knowledge often results in a correspondent having to write to an old aunt or some one else who is far away, for definite data. And presumably the aunt has to write, when she gets around to it, to a sister in some other place, perhaps a remote corner of the country, to help out. Weeks and sometimes months go by without any reply, leaving the genealogist uncertain whether any attempt is being made to assist him.

A correspondent may know some family history and have every intention to help by answering letters addressed to him or filling in information on Work Sheets sent him, but the busy life of the ordinary person makes it easy to lay aside such matters until some more convenient time for answering which is, usually, never. He does not realize that the genealogist is probably spending valuable time and hundreds of dollars trying to get answers to those inquiries that are so nonchalantly laid aside for a more convenient season.

Another reason for unsatisfactory replies is indefiniteness. It is the usual experience to have a large correspondence with many people who try their best to help, but who do not know how to give definite information, and therefore write long letters that, while interesting, are totally devoid of information or data. This interesting correspondence would be delightful were it not for the fact that any one who undertakes to write a genealogy is the busiest person imaginable, buried with necessary correspondence, and usually too poorly paid to afford secretarial assistance.

The correspondent does not realize that the genealogist has very meagre knowledge of the branch of the family about which he is making inquiry. Matters that are so thoroughly known to the correspondent are assumed to be somewhat familiar to the genealogist. This may be illustrated by the experience of a compiler with an old lady in a midwestern city recently. She replied to his letters promptly with abundant references to "my husband," "my son in Detroit," "my son's wife," "my grandchildren," "my sister's oldest boy," etc., but not one name or date in her whole letter. She did not answer a single question that had been asked, and evidently did not reread the letter of inquiry at the time she was answering it. This was repeated three times, and then she was sent a Work Sheet with such information as was at hand filled in, and asked to complete and return the identical blank. It came back promptly, properly completed, and gave all the desired information that six months of correspondence had failed to secure.

A word should be said regarding family tradition as it enters into correspondence. Tradition may be proved to be fact, but often it is otherwise, and sometimes it is very difficult to weed out tradition from among the facts. This is particularly true in correspondence. Some one says to his children, "Grandfather *was said* to have come from Rhode Island," and years later one of those children, who is sought for information on this subject writes: "Father *said* his grandfather came from Rhode Island." That was not what the father said at all. Later it may be found that he did come from Rhode Island, or it may have been Connecticut from which he came. Tradition, in being repeated, was stated as fact. This sort of misinformation is often exceedingly difficult to catch and correct, and every correspondent should be cautioned to qualify all information he is not absolutely sure about, by stating his source of knowledge or reason for belief.

Tradition has its place in genealogy as a suggestive source of information. When a letter is received from a western correspondent saying that the family was supposed to have come from "Little Rock, Rhode Island," and there is no Little Rock in Rhode Island, and never was so far as is known, the suggestion at once prompts a search in Kingston which in the early days was known by the name of Little Rest, or in Lime Rock, a neighborhood in the town of Lincoln, for the family, with possible satisfactory results. Therefore it cannot be said that the family tradition is worthless and is to be entirely avoided in genealogical work, but it must be used with the greatest of caution. It is a guess that must be investigated and either proved or disproved, or else it must be clearly branded in the record as tradition.

How To Prepare Field Papers

In using the same form of Working Sheets for Field Working Papers, such data as the genealogist has should be inserted in its proper place and preferably with a typewriter. This start will be encouraging to whoever is to receive and attempt to complete it. If it is done either with a typewriter, or with a color of ink not commonly used, any additions or

NO	INDEX
2746	aabdc ac

NAME
    *Ruth Turner

FATHER'S NAME
    Ezekiel Turner

MOTHER'S NAME
    *Ruth Randall

BORN AT   ON   1828

DIED AT   ON

MARRIED AT   ON

TO
    Micah Sylvester

FATHER'S NAME

MOTHER'S NAME

BORN AT   ON

DIED AT   ON

RESIDENCE

OCCUPATION

BIOGRAPHY

alterations by the correspondent will be quickly discernable. In typewriting it is advisable not to use a black ribbon which is the color so universally used today, but some color that will contrast with any work the correspondent may elect to do with the ordinarily equipped machine.

The partially filled in sheet should bear the same Progressive Number as the one from which it is copied in the genealogist's file, and when returned and indexed, it should be filed with the original. In typing it, a carbon copy should be taken which may be on cheap unprinted paper, as its only use will be to keep a check on the Work Sheets sent out until such time as they are returned. These copies should be filed by number in cheap manilla envelopes, on which should be written the Progressive Numbers appearing on the sheets enclosed, the name and address of the person to whom they are sent, and the date on which they go out, thus:

Nos. 2746, 2747, 2748, 2749
Mrs. J. Thomas Wilbur, 235 Main St., Yonkers, N. Y.
4/8/1931

In this way it is easy to know what, when and from whom information has been sought, and if answers are not received within a reasonable time it is easy to follow up with further correspondence.

Inasmuch as some explanation is necessary to go with the Field Working Papers being sent out, a printed letter can be enclosed with it. Something on the order of the following is suggested:

OFFICE OF THE GENEALOGIST OF THE
CHILDS FAMILY IN AMERICA
23 MAIN ST.
BEVERLY, MASSACHUSETTS

Dear Cousin:

To complete the history of the family of Thomas Childs who came to America in 1634 and settled in Duxbury, Massachusetts, information is being sought.

Enclosed you will find a form which we have filled out so far as we have information. Will you kindly check this data for correctness, and add as much as possible of the required information, and return the sheet to this office. Return postage is enclosed, and as these sheets are numbered, please do not destroy or keep them, but return them as soon as possible that we may not be unnecessarily delayed with the work.

We wish to use one of these sheets for each descendant having children. If you need more of the sheets please send a list of descendants who have, or have left, families, and sheets will be forwarded to you.

If you cannot furnish the information sought, please return the sheet and send us the name and address of any one who can help us.

We are preparing a very valuable genealogy at great expense, and we depend on you to co-operate with us in every way that you can. It is your work as well as ours.

Very sincerely yours,

Such a letter is very helpful in securing replies. It has seemed, when used, to be as satisfactory as a written letter, and saves greatly both in time and labor.

Small as it may seem, many people will not spend the necessary money for a postage stamp for a reply. Therefore it is suggested that the genealogist adopt the government plan of using Business Reply Envelopes. While there is an extra cent rate on this class of mail it is only payable on those replies which are returned, and no postage is wasted on those who do not reply. The cost of this plan is less than that of enclosing stamped envelopes.

To secure the permit for the use of these envelopes, it is only necessary to apply through the post office through which in-coming mail is to be received, and when the permit is issued, which is done without cost, any local printer can furnish the printed envelopes as specified in the post office regulations. It has been found that enclosing these paid reply envelopes greatly assists in securing the desired information. It is often advisable to send duplicate blanks to various members of the family. While one may know one date, another will know some other necessary information. Duplicates should all bear the same Progressive Number so that they may be filed together upon their return.

INDEXING WORKING PAPERS

Indexing is a tedious task and an easy one to neglect, but in no line of work is a carefully made index of greater importance than in the preparation of a genealogy. Unless the genealogist is untiring in his indexing, he will soon find himself consulting books that he has already examined and from which he has abstracted; writing people for information which is already in his files; duplicating his work in various directions. It is entirely impossible for him to remember what he has or has not done, when he is going over names by the tens of thousands, and if he could remember it would be a useless mental exercise. The successful genealogist must index early and late, everlastingly index, but do it in such a way that it will most speedily and successfully accomplish its purpose.

For every index needed in the entire proposition, the best card to use is what is commonly known as Library size

(2 x 5). It is as large as is necessary and is better than the ordinary 3 x 5 card as it saves an inch both in cost and in filing space which is worth consideration. Index cards of this size can most cheaply be cut from sheet stock by any printer and should cost around a dollar per thousand if cut from cover stock which is thinner and tougher than the cheaper grades of card stock.

To distinguish easily different indexes, different colors should be used, white for Working Sheets, primrose for the book index, gray for a mailing list, etc. By this arrangement there is little liability of confusing the different indexes.

Two indexes are advisable for the Work Sheets. A general index which should embrace every name written, and be so made as to make clear from the index without consulting the Work Sheets which particular person of the same name is wanted. This is especially necessary because of the constant recurrence of old family names such as John, Thomas, Mary, Abigail, etc. These names will run through generation after generation and unless there is some way to tell from the index which John or which Abigail is wanted, the genealogist will find himself getting out from his files envelope after envelope of Work Sheets on which the wanted name appears as shown by the index. It is surprising how many times these Work Sheets will have to be consulted as information keeps coming in from all sources.

It is suggested that the general index of Work Sheets be made thus:

<pre>
       *Jacobs, Grace M.   1873-1897
       of *John H. and Mary E. (Sampson) Jacobs
       m. George R. Hill
       Rockland, Mass.
       2958
</pre>

This gives the name; the approximate date of birth and death (the dash following the year of birth as 1826-; preceding the date of death as -1874; separating the dates of birth and death if both are known as 1826-1874; and preceding and following where birth and death occur in the same year as -1874-); the name of the parents which will be found useful; the name of the husband or wife as the case may be; and if known, some place of residence either at birth or later in life where information is most likely to be found.

When the index is consulted for any information of Grace M. Jacobs, born about 1873, there is no question what Grace M. Jacobs is wanted even though there be a dozen of the same name in the genealogy. The story is all on the index, and Work Sheet No. 2958 is the only one that needs to be removed from the files. There is of course no other Grace M. Jacobs in the entire index with the same distinguishing data on her index card. It is well also to continue the practice of starring of checking the name in line of the blood.

In the case of in-laws the index merely says:

> Sampson, William
> m. Mary Russell
> 2958

There being no asterisk or check it is understood that William Sampson was merely a parent of an in-law and not properly a part of the genealogy.

The practice of so carefully and explicitly indexing will be attacked on the ground of time and labor involved, but the genealogist has only to make the test of finding a member by this method and then one by that of simple indexing by name and number of sheet to convince himself of its value and saving qualities. With the Work Sheets properly filed as will be later explained it should not take over thirty seconds to find any particular person in an index of forty thousand names.

If there are several Work Sheets having information of the same person, they may be all indexed on the same card or a new card may be made for each time the name appears on a different Work Sheet. The latter method will consume more cards and fill the index file faster thus requiring more filing room, but will take far less time than examining the index each time the name is found, and on the whole will be found the more satisfactory plan.

To avoid double indexing, the name appearing in the heading of the sheet and the name of the husband or wife with the father-in-law and mother-in-law should be indexed. The names of the father and mother of the subject having been previously indexed on their own sheet, they should not be done again. In indexing children, those names marked for continuation should not be indexed on their father's and mother's Work Sheet, but will be indexed when picked up on their own Work Sheets in continuation. All uncontinued names of children should be indexed on the parent's sheet, together with the names of any family appearing with them.

INDEX GUIDES

Guide cards may be easily made from the same cover stock having them cut one fourth inch wider (2¼ x 5) and printing the name or index subdivision of the alphabet on the very top edge of the card so that it will be visible above the edge of the regular cards. A separate color should be used for guide cards, varying the color if subindexes are to be used. The alphabet may be divided on the guide cards to meet the requirements, which is an advantage over the stock cards on the market. If the genealogy is to index a large number of names it will be found advantageous to put in a guide card headed with each given name of the family surname, as Aaron, Abigail etc. and separate guide cards for each surname other than that of the family under consideration, as Aaronson, Abbe, Anderson, etc. This will require more cards than the regular subdivision of the alphabet, but it will greatly speed up the finding of names as they are wanted in the work, and if a hard finished fifty pound stock is used it will not unduly fill up the files.

Indexing Variations of Spelling Surnames

In indexing Work Sheets it is not advisable to index surnames by their various spellings, as Whiton-Whiting, Haines-Haynes, Munro-Munroe-Monroe, etc. The most commonly used form of spelling should be selected and adhered to throughout the work. Unless this is done mistakes are likely to occur because all of the variations may not be examined. There seems to be no law to prevent any member of the Smith family from adopting Smythe as the way he spells his name. When nearly all the other members of the family spell the name Smith it is easy to forget to look under Smythe, nor is it conducive to speed and ease of work if the genealogist has always to look under Smythe when looking up the Smiths to be sure that he has not missed some one. A cross reference card should be made for each form of spelling and filed in its proper place. If the spelling Smythe is found in the work, the index card should simply read: Smythe—See Smith. The index card of the particular Smythe should be written Smythe, however, but filed under Smith. This should only

NO.		INDEX	
2874		ahaji cg	

NAME
*Alvin Studley

FATHER'S NAME
*Nathan Studley

MOTHER'S NAME
Huldah Ellis

BORN AT East Abington **ON** 9/25/1819

DIED AT **ON**

MARRIED AT **ON** 6/ /1842

TO Mercy B. Ellis

FATHER'S NAME William Ellis

MOTHER'S NAME Bethia Josselyn

BORN AT **ON** 12/3/1824

DIED AT **ON**

RESIDENCE

OCCUPATION

BIOGRAPHY

AUTHORITY
Hanover p.389

apply to the index of Work Sheets. In the index made for the printed book, all forms of spelling should be placed in their proper order in the index.

Dropped Lines on Working Papers

About as soon as Work Papers are begun the problem of what to do with incomplete blanks presents itself. In the examination of a town history it will be found that a family in line is carried to the history of the father and mother and the names and dates of the births of the children, but there the history ends the family. The incomplete history of these children creates what is termed Dropped Lines. It is also often found that only certain children of a family are carried along with their individual families while other members are dropped with no information as to what became of them; whether they married and had families or died without families. All of these incomplete histories must be given attention and some method must be provided for Dropped Lines.

It will be seen that Clara L. Studley, the first child of this union, is not carried forward in the Hanover History. She was born in 1844 and may, or may not, have had a family of her own. She must be dropped here so far as this source of information goes, but more information is wanted of her. If this sheet is kept out of the files for continuation it is lost for reference, not only as regards Clara L., but the whole family of her father. This must not be allowed. Files must not be broken up. It would soon be discovered that the continuation sheet exceeded those in the files which were complete,

4 CHILDREN

---

(1) NAME **Clara L. Studley**

BORN AT **East Abington, Mass.** ON **5/25/1844**

DIED AT ON

MARRIED AT ON

TO

---

(2) NAME **George E. Studley**

BORN AT **(3047)** ON **6/30/1846**

DIED AT ON

MARRIED AT ON

TO

---

(3) NAME **Chas. J. Studley**

BORN AT **East Abington** ON **5/25/1848**

DIED AT **(3048)** ON

MARRIED AT ON

TO

---

(4) NAME **John M. Studley**

BORN AT **East Abington** ON **5/18/1850**

DIED AT **(3049)** ON

MARRIED AT ON

TO

---

and the file would be utterly useless. All the work that has been done must quickly be available for comparison and consultation. To overcome this difficulty a plain sheet should be used for continuation. It should be on thin tough paper and should be cut three and three quarters by six and three quarters inches and punched to fit the stock ring binder that it may be carried in a binder when in use. There is no need for printing on these sheets. The continuation sheet should be typed and a carbon copy taken, the use of which will be explained later. The subject matter on the sheet should be:

> Studley   2874
> Abington, Mass.
> Hanover History 389
> *Clara L. Studley 1844-
> of Alvin and Mercy B. (Josselyn)
> Studley.

The remainder of the sheet is left blank, on which can be made notes and references as found relating to Clara L. This heading will furnish the name to be used in further search, the name of the town where examination is to be made, the name of the source of information, and where she was dropped, Hanover History p. 389; in fact, all the information which has been secured about her. Her father's Work Sheet can now be filed for reference as it may be needed.

The original of this continuation sheet is now filed in an envelope which is marked "For Investigation." All continuation sheets where the surname begins with S. can be filed together, or if there are enough sheets to warrant it, there may be an envelope for Studley alone. This filing may be made as elastic as the needs require.

By using thin sheets for continuation many of them can be carried in a ring binder for use in libraries or wherever the genealogist is working.

When further information is found relating to Clara L. Studley her name is transferred to a Work Sheet and she is given a Progressive Number; her father's Work Sheet, No. 2874, is taken from the files and in her blank at the top of the page containing the names of his children, is inserted her Progressive Number, and on her Work Sheet in the Reference line is marked 2874, her father's Work Sheet number, thereby tying the record of the parent in line to that of the child.

In the case of daughters who married and were dropped after marriage, the continuation sheet should be filed under the letter of the husband's surname. If Clara L. had married Robert Jones and her history had ended there in Hanover p. 389, the continuation sheet would have been made thus:

> Jones 2874
> Abington, Mass.
> Hanover p. 389
> *Clara L. Studley 1844-
> of *Alvin and Mercy B. (Josselyn)
> Studley
> m. Robert Jones.

It would be filed under J. or Jones in its proper envelope. It is not advisable to file over twenty-five sheets in an envelope. Many sheets out of an envelope at one time lead to confusion of papers liability of loss, and waste of time in sorting and arranging again in proper order.

TOWN AND STATE FILE

The carbon copy of the above sheet now serves as a Town and State file. It is noted in the illustration that Alvin Studley and his daughter, Clara L., were both born in East Abington, Massachusetts, and that more information is wanted regarding them. East Abington, which is a section of the town of Abington, must be kept in mind in relation to this particular family.

This carbon copy should be filed in an envelope marked Abington, Mass. and placed in a Town and State list in its proper alphabetical place under Massachusetts. As the work progresses there will be wanted information from the same town relative to other persons, and the Abington envelope will be gradually filled with continuation sheets where more information is needed. The Abington envelope will contain continuation sheets for every person in the entire project where it is believed information can be found in that town. If this list is not made the genealogist will find himself someday in Abington and ready for work that he knows must be done there, realizing that there are many things in his investigations that he needs to look up there, but with no remembrance what they were or where in his multitude of papers they are to be found. The actual work of making this Town and State file is nil as it is only a carbon copy of the continuation sheet which is cross filed by town instead of by surname.

Correspondence Index

The Work Sheet should be looked over once more before it is filed away, to see if there are addresses of any one who, by the laws of natural life, should be living at the present time. If any one is found in this way it is a source of further information. It is suggested that these names and addresses be indexed and filed by States and Towns as possible family contacts. If subsequent correspondence proves the supposition that the person is alive, his name should be underscored in blue, and if it later develops that he is a correspondent who can be relied upon to help with the work by furnishing data and information, the name should be underscored again in red. Thus is gradually built up a correspondence list of hundreds of names that are points of contact for help, which is of inestimable value.

The genealogist may lose a family from the records, the last known of them being that they were living in San Diego, California in 1890. By consulting his correspondence index he finds that he has a correspondent in San Diego who has expressed a willingness to be of assistance. A letter to this correspondent, with a Work Sheet to complete, may very probably bring the desired information and add an entire family to the genealogy with the expenditure of two postage stamps. No way could be easier or cheaper.

It must be borne in mind also that while these hundreds of people are helping in this small way with the compilation of the genealogy, they are developing an interest which will very probably lead to the purchase of the published work, and a sale is necessary to provide funds for the printing of genealogies.

FILING THE WORK SHEETS

The genealogist is now ready to file the Work Sheet. These sheets should be filed in numerical order as indicated by the Progressive Numbers, in stiff manila envelopes, commonly called by the trade "Number Ten." There should not be over fifty, and preferably not over twenty-five, sheets in an envelope as there will be additions from time to time as Field Work Sheets come in bearing duplicate numbers.

The same size envelope should be used for filing continuation sheets, both by surname and by town and state. The envelope will stand constant use and wear well and it fits the regular stock document filing case, also the regular size document tin can which, if the compiler is using an automobile for his field work, is an excellent method for carrying papers for outside investigation. Two of these cans will carry five thousand Work Sheets or Continuation Sheets in their envelopes, instantly available as needed. There can be carried the continuation sheets for a whole state in a handbag, all readily accessible and safe from confusion. The file is not disturbed; it is merely carried with the worker wherever his work leads him, and when he returns to his own office is ready for reference in connection with his indexes as quickly as though it had not been removed from its accustomed place in the office.

Continuation sheets should be thrown away as soon as information regarding the person to whom they refer has been secured. They have then served their purpose and are of no more use.

By following through this working plan it will be found that a maximum amount of work can be accomplished with a minimum amount of duplication, and thereby time and labor can be conserved.

CHAPTER FIVE : *PROBLEMS*

THE compilation of a genealogy or family history would be exceedingly prosaic and totally lacking in spice if there were no problems to be encountered in the work. To copy names and dates from first one book and then another and piece the data together might, like a puzzle, provide interest for a time, but that sort of task soon grows wearisome. It would not be sufficiently interesting to keep a genealogist at his work over a period of several years to the conclusion of his task.

The genealogist cannot change the history of an individual or of a family, and it would seem at first thought that his only activity is that of a copyist and an editor with no opportunity for mental exercise other than a knowledge of the methods of compilation coupled with an ability to use good English, and a spirit of exactness.

There is, however, another side to the work. The genealogist must just as truly be a creator as is the novelist, in fact, more so. The story writer can dream and, whether his dream be probable does not matter. He is not bothered with proving anything. Often times the more improbable his creation, the more fascinating is his story and the greater his success as a writer and a story teller.

The genealogist, however, must be a theorist. He must create a story and then labor hard and long to prove that his theory is not only a story, but a true story.

Genealogy, like every other science, has its element of problem, of experimentation and of mystery. The successful genealogist must be a man of vision and a guesser. He must be able to see two and two making five, and then go out and find the missing one that makes the five a fact. But he must not forget that he has to find that one and he must never assume that it is somewhere hidden away and can be taken for granted. It must be hunted up and brought out to the light, turned about and looked at until there is no doubt that it is the particular one that is wanted.

Many occasions will arise during the compilation of the work where it will be concluded that a connection must exist between an obscure line and the main family, but where there is no positive proof to substantiate such a conclusion. If the record of a birth, marriage or death is not to be found, there is nothing to do about it but accept the fact that there is no record. If the fact cannot be established by private record, and there is not even tradition upon which to base a conclusion, there is only one thing left to do, and that is to attempt to build up the case by cumulative evidence.

It will be found in these obscure families that old family names occur repeatedly. They may be odd and unfamiliar names like that of "Zattu" in the Cushing family. By some such indication there is created in the mind of the genealogist a suspicion of a family connection, which thought finally becomes a belief of certainty, but there is no proof at hand.

In those families where there has been found but one emigrant ancestor bearing the same surname it is pretty certain that all those bearing the same surname are sprung from that common ancestor. It is not always safe to assume this however. There are three exceptions which should be guarded against in this assumption. First. If any of the family were slave holders it must be remembered that slaves, if they had a surname, usually took that of their masters. This must be especially watched in instances where members of the family settled in the South many years ago. The genealogist must not be surprised to find negro families bearing his surname. Second. There has always been a tendency on the part of foreign people with unpronounceable names when they settled in America to change either or both given names or surnames without leave or license, adopting any one that suggested itself as most useful for business or other reasons. For this reason the genealogist may find a family of Italians, Armenians or Russian Jews with a surname of one of the old colonial families. Third. It must not be overlooked that the early emigrant was only one of the many in the homeland bearing the same surname, and that those who did not migrate at that time have gone on raising families, some one or more of whom may have come to America in more recent years. In the cases of old New England families ship lists and migrations are not usually checked after the ancestor is found, but that does not mean that some bearing the family name have not emigrated during a later time.

In obscure lines it is difficult to establish the fact that all bearing the same surname are from a common ancestor even though there is found evidence of only one emigrant.

The spirit of adventure which prompted so many to leave England in the days of settlement to investigate a new land in America has always been present as an element of human nature. It drove men tramping into the wilderness of the "west" when that west was only as far away as the frontier of New York state; it drove families transported by ox teams to the central states; it drove adventurous gold seekers to the Pacific coast in 1849. It was the same human element of adventure that prompted men in recent times to seek the ice covered poles of the earth. It is a spirit as old as humanity and it will manifest itself as long as men live.

The genealogist will be told of an adventurous son of the family who "went west and was never heard from again." Doubtless some of these sons died of hardship, but it is probable that many more of them finally found wives from among the settlers whom they met in their travels, and they lived to old age, rearing families. Many times there can be found no record of these families because there was not even a town organization in which there could be clerks to keep records even if they had been so disposed.

The memory of their descendants may reach back and furnish the desired link, but this is not always possible and the genealogist is bound to find many families with no suggestion as to their connection with the main family. If the line is brought into its proper kinship it must be done by circumstantial evidence.

The question arises as to whether circumstantial evidence is sufficient to warrant assuming that its sum total establishes fact. In answer to this it must be cited that the courts have agreed that a man's life may be saved or sacrificed by such evidence. Very often in criminal practice no one person knows any particular fact upon which the innocence or conviction of a person under trial can be established, but it is the accumulation of facts, insignificant in themselves when considered alone, which are gathered from many sources, which are built up, piece by piece, until there is a structure so strong that courts feel justified in taking a man's liberty away from him, and in some instances, taking his very life itself.

If evidence of this sort is sufficient to free or hang a man, it certainly should be sufficient for the admission of a line into the body of a family.

No genealogy has ever been written in which there did not arise many instances where the family connection must be established by cumulative evidence. Such cases are difficult to handle and require the most painstaking work of any that the genealogist will be called upon to perform. They usually present themselves in the early period of the work. And because they are of early origin the fate of a large number of people and of individual families will depend upon their settlement. At the present period in American families descended from colonial ancestors the ninth and tenth generations are mostly the ones living. It will readily be seen that any question effecting the third or fourth generations would either include or exclude a great many people.

Occasions will be met where there is no evidence that can be found that will prove, even circumstantially, a family connection, in which case the only thing the genealogist can do is to put the disconnected family in an appendix and simply make the statement that while the family probably came from the same common ancestor as those of the other branches in the compilation, there has been found no proof of its connection. It is always disappointing to be obliged to do this as it appears like a confession on the part of the genealogist that he has failed somewhat in the accomplishment of his task. The family so segregated is bound to feel somewhat slighted and, while its members are not able to furnish proof of the connecting link themselves, they seem to feel that the genealogist, who is a specialist in his line of work, should have possessed some superhuman insight that would have revealed to him things not visible to the laity.

Problem of American Origin

The occasion may arise where the common ancestor is found in some early American settlement with no record from whence he came or the ship by which he reached America. These instances are not rare. They were caused quite likely by the educational limits of the early times.

It is found that one of the most prominent men of the Plymouth Colony could not read or write. He was a delegate to many meetings for the settlement of serious controversies among the colonists; between those of the Plymouth Plantation and those of the Massachusetts Bay, and between the colonists and the Indians. He established town boundaries, helped to establish the boundary between the Plymouth and the Massachusetts Bay colonies, laid out and apportioned the common lands, and for a great many years was one of the most useful men of the Plymouth Colony settlement. It is not known, however, when he came to America. While he could not read or write he appears not to have suffered very much thereby in establishing his place in the community, and he probably was one of the large majority who had little or no education from books, and whose only education was that of a naturally bright mind instructed by experience and observation.

He was found in Scituate, Massachusetts in 1634, but there is no record of how he got there. He was probably one of the "Men of Kent" who came with the Rev. John Lothrop in that year. He may have been one of the earlier comers. That his name does not appear on any of the ship lists may be accounted for by the fact that he could not write it himself, and in pronouncing it, whoever made the list of passengers for the ship in which he came, wrote down what he thought was the name from hearing it pronounced. There is little doubt but that a name intended to be his is on the list of some ship which came into Plymouth Harbor between 1620 and the end of 1634, but what that name was and how it was written and where it is to be found is a question to be solved.

It is not a long period to search—only fourteen years—and not many ships, comparatively speaking, came to Plymouth Bay during those years. The genealogist should examine every one of those ships lists with an imaginative mind. First, for names which sound like the one wanted. Let him pronounce the name and imagine with the English accent, possibly with Scotch accent, what a total stranger writing it down would most likely put on the book. Then he should go over the lists for elimination. There is certain knowledge regarding the after life of many of those who came in the early ships. Each name should be taken and eliminated if the subsequent history of the passenger can be established. Those names can be then crossed off and the list narrowed down to a handful from which must be found the solution of the problem. It will probably appear that some one who came apparently disappeared from history and the connection can thus be established between a passenger who was lost from the record and an ancestor who was found with no record of ever having been a passenger to America.

PROBLEM OF EMIGRANT MARRIAGE

Closely connected with the problem of missing names on ship lists is that of whether the emigrant came as a single man or was married before arriving in America. If the given name of the wife of the emigrant ancestor is known it may help very much in finding the couple on the ship list provided they were married before the emigration. If two given names were connected as husband and wife on the list and it is recognized that those were the given names of the ancestors, the case is strengthened.

The business of raising a family was strictly attended to in colonial times and for several generations thereafter. Because of this it is fairly easy to establish a probable date of marriage from the date of birth of the first child if that is known. Raising a family was well regulated. Seldom did more than a year elapse between marriage and the birth of a child, and each second year thereafter saw a new addition in the family with almost clocklike regularity.

Following the illustration of the Scituate settler referred to above, who was found in that town in 1634, it is not known when he married or the surname of his wife. It is known, however, that while he was in Scituate in 1634, his first child was not born until 1639, five years after we have found record of the father. It is fair to presume, therefore, that the emigrant was not married when he came to America, and instead of looking for a man and wife linked together on a ship list, whose given names are known, search should be made for a stray woman listed as unmarried and bearing the given name of the one who was later known to have been the wife of the emigrant.

In this case it is not known what her surname was, therefore it cannot be determined whether she was correctly listed on the ship's list or not. All that is known on which to base the search is her given name. Here also there is room for mistake. In the case recited years were spent searching for a woman passenger by the name of Hannah, only to discover that her name was Honour and not Hannah. If the family name of the wife can be found it may unearth the information wanted regarding the husband.

If the given name of either husband or wife is known, all names on the ship lists bearing the same given name should be scrutinized. Every bit of information should be examined with the utmost care, and every clue run to earth. In all these matters the genealogist must have a lively imagination, and have it well under control that it does not run away with him and arrive at a determination from such imagination rather than from the weight of evidence.

Problem of Early Lost Lines

In the early generations members of the family were not infrequently lost in their removal from one of the New England states to another or from one section to another in

the same state. This was particularly common in the removals to Maine when that territory was a part of Massachusetts and mostly wilderness wherein settlements were
being established. In later generations, members were lost
by going to the western frontier which was the western portion
of New York state. From these settlements they were lost as
they pushed westward into the new country of the now
Central States, and it is within the memory of those living
today when relatives were lost in the wilderness west of the
Mississippi River.

In order to understand better this problem of lost members it is necessary to remember that the means of communication were very limited as compared with those of today.
There was no telephone or telegraph and letters were dependent on slow travel from point to point for many hundreds
of miles. In the early settlements there was no regular mail
service, letters getting in to the settlement when someone
came in from the older settlements, and going out at the
convenience of some traveler who, tiring of the hardships,
turned his face back east, or someone going out for supplies,
which was seldom.

It must be borne in mind that the member of the family
with the roving and pioneering disposition was not usually
the scholar of the family, but the reverse. Many times the
migrant had not the ability to write home even if he had
possessed the disposition to do so. The wonder is not that so
many young men who "went west" were lost to their families who stayed in the old home in the east, but that more of
them were not swallowed up in the wilderness and never
heard from again by their relatives.

Perhaps the best method of explaining cumulative evidence in finding lost members of a family is to take a typical case and carry it through.

It is found that Cornelius Robinson settled in one of the southern Rhode Island towns, and that he married Thankful Saunders in 1733. There is record of their having had seven children, viz.:

> Elizabeth
> Freegift, b. June 26, 1738
> Sarah, b. Oct. 2, 1740
> Hannah, b. Nov. 1742
> Ruth, b. Mar. 27, 1745
> Stephen, b. May 17, 1747 and
> Cornelius, b. Aug. 7, 1749.

The birth date of Elizabeth is not recorded, but when she married she was published as the daughter of Cornelius and Thankful. She married in 1753, which was twenty years after the marriage of her father and mother. She was probably their first child, born in 1734 and was nineteen years old at the time of her marriage.

The next child of whom there is any record was Freegift who was born in 1738. She was born presumably four years after Elizabeth. By all the rules of raising families in that day, there should have been a child born in 1736. It will be noted that in the subsequent record of births in the family there was a child about every two years. The four year period between the probable birth of Elizabeth and the known date of the birth of Freegift causes suspicion that there was another child whose birth was not recorded, and about whom there was no other record, born in 1736. It may have been a child who died in infancy, but whatever became of the child that period must be accounted for in some way. Of course it may have been possible that a first child died and was never recorded, but that would bring the marriage of Elizabeth to seventeen years of age. All indications are that there is a place for a birth in this family in 1736.

The next step is to ascertain if there was subsequently found any one of the same name in the vicinity whose parentage could not be accounted for by the records. If so, can sufficient evidence be produced to lead to the conclusion that the parents of that child may have been Cornelius and Thankful?

A new line of evidence is started and it is found by private record that one Thomas Robinson was born in the same town and that the names of his parents are not known. It is known, however, that he married in the same town in January of 1758, Mary Hall; that in his marriage publication he was recited as being a resident of the town; that he was married by Stephen Saunders, a Justice of the Peace, and a brother of Thankful Saunders who had married Cornelius Robinson of that place. It was also found that Stephen Saunders married three other of the children of his sister Thankful, among whom was Stephen who married Dorcas Hall.

It is found too, that Cornelius was the son of Isaac, who was the son of Robert, who had a brother Thomas, so that Thomas was a family name as was also Isaac. In following the subsequent history of the family it is discovered that Thomas who married Mary Hall had a grandchild named Isaac, one named Robert and one named Thomas and that all of these family names, together with many other of the names appearing in the family of Cornelius have been repeated in the descendants of Thomas down to the present generation.

If Thomas who married Mary Hall in 1758 had been the son of Cornelius and Thankful, born in 1736, he would have been twenty-two years old at the time of his marriage, which would have been a proper age for that event to have taken place; he would have been married by his uncle Stephen as were three of his brothers and sisters, and his wife, Mary Hall, may quite probably have been the sister of Dorcas Hall who married his brother Stephen.

Thus it would seem that Thomas was the son of Cornelius and Thankful; that he was their second child, and that he was born in 1736.

Leaving the family there, the next move is to learn if there is any evidence of any other Thomas Robinson in that locality between 1725 and 1760. No record can be found of a Thomas, or even of another Robinson family in the records of that town or of any other of the surrounding towns. There appears to be no other way to account for Thomas unless he can be injected into this vacant period in the family of Cornelius and Thankful. Thus both by positive and adverse evidence it must be concluded that Thomas was the son of Cornelius and Thankful and that he was born in 1736.

The point to determine is, having arrived at this conclusion, shall it be written into the history as fact and thus have a place in the family and be dismissed from any further consideration. While the evidence seems strong enough to place the family of Thomas in the line of that of Cornelius, it should be done only after proper explanation of the process by which the conclusion is reached that the correct place has been found for Thomas. The evidence is too strong to exclude the family and place it in an appendix, but on the other hand it is a conclusion based on cumulative evidence rather than on facts of record and should be so stated.

The problem of placing Thomas in the family has been settled by finding room for him in the family of Cornelius and Thankful. The subsequent family of Thomas, however, presents another and a more difficult problem. He married Mary Hall in January of 1758. By custom there should have been a child born of the union during the latter part of 1758 or early in 1759. There are known to be two children born to Thomas and Mary, the birth of only one of whom is recorded. The first of these children was Susan who was known to have been born in 1769, eleven years after the marriage of her father and mother. She married in December of 1787. It is doubtful if she was the first child of the family. The only other child, whose birth was recorded, born to Thomas and Mary, was Benjamin who was born in 1772, three years after the birth of his sister Susan, which probably places him as the next child in the family. The eleven year period between marriage and the birth of Susan, however, shows altogether too much family irregularity to have been the entire history of the union. It would seem that there must have been children born to the parents before Susan. Considering the infant mortality of those early times it may be quite possible that there were a number of children born during this period who did not survive and whose births and deaths did not get on any record.

It is known that Susan and Benjamin both married and removed from Rhode Island to Franklin County, Massachusetts where they settled and spent the remainder of their lives on adjoining farms each having raised a large family. Of Susan's ten children, several were born before their removal from Rhode Island, and of Benjamin's family of eleven children, four are known to have been born before the family came to Franklin County. This places the removal of the families as around 1800.

Now, to leave Susan and Benjamin for the time being. There is found another family of the same surname in the same vicinity in southern Rhode Island, and because, when we attempted to place the parentage of Thomas there was found no other family of the name there, it must be concluded that there is a connection between this new family and that of Cornelius and Thomas.

The given name of the father of this family is not known, but it is known that he married Nancy Briggs, and that beginning with 1801 this couple had a family of ten children. Whether the father and mother of this family ever went to Franklin County, Massachusetts is not known. Three of their sons went there and settled in an adjoining town to that in which Susan and Benjamin were living. In this family of ten children there appear the names of Freegift, Saunders and Thomas, all of which are familiar family names. The first child of this family was born in 1801 which places the probable date of marriage as around 1800 and the approximate birth of the father as around 1775. Inasmuch as there was no other family of the name found in the vicinity from which this man could have sprung, it would indicate that he was another child of Thomas and Mary and younger than Benjamin.

The question arises why three of the sons of this family went to Franklin County, Massachusetts, and settled near Susan and Benjamin unless there was a family connection. Were Susan and Benjamin their aunt and uncle? For whom was Freegift named unless for the aunt of her father? The name is not common in the family and is found in no other branch. For whom was Saunders named unless it was for the family of grandmother Thankful? And is it not clear that Thomas was named for his grandfather, Thomas, and as the name of his father is not known, that also may have been Thomas. There was a Nancy named for her mother.

To continue this interesting investigation, is to go from one problem to a still deeper one. John, Briggs and Saunders went to Franklin County, Massachusetts and settled, from which place, after a little time, they migrated to the western part of New York, not far from where Buffalo now stands. They were all young men and unmarried. Shortly Briggs and Saunders tired of the hardship and returned to Franklin County, leaving John alone in New York. Briggs married, and after the birth of his first child, he, with his family and Saunders returned to New York state to find John. They never found him.

Later the other seven children of the family all went to western New York where they settled, married and had families. Whether they went directly from Rhode Island; whether they went by way of Franklin County, Massachusetts; whether the father and mother ever left Rhode Island, is not known.

Years later a large family was found in the northwest corner of Pennsylvania and the eastern part of Ohio who said they were the descendents of one John, whose ancestry none of the family knew, nor did they know from what place he came, but there was a family tradition that he came from Rhode Island.

Whether he was the same John who went from Rhode Island to Franklin County, Massachusetts, and on with Briggs and Saunders to western New York is not known, which in itself presents a genealogical problem.

There now appears to have been located a possible third child of Thomas and Mary. There was Susan who was born eleven years after the marriage of her father and mother, Benjamin who was born three years after Susan, and possibly another son whose name is not known, but who was younger than Benjamin. Still there is the matter of those years before the birth of Susan. Were there other children who reared families that have not been found? If there were other children and their families were the size of those of Susan and Benjamin—twenty-one children—and a possibility of a family of ten more from a son of unknown name, there is yet much for the genealogist to do to gather in the stray progeny of Thomas and Mary.

What shall be done about this unnamed member of the family with his children, the names of whom are so suggestive? Is there strong enough evidence that they are of the family of Thomas and Mary to warrant putting them in there with an explanation? It would hardly seem that the case has been proved beyond a reasonable doubt. It is very suggestive, but the name of Freegift may have come from another family. Stephen Saunders married many couples and any number of them may have been grateful enough to name a child for him. Thomas was a quite common name of the times. Coming from the same town it might not be surprising that these three boys went to Franklin County where they might be near old neighbors, though no relation. The fact that no other Robinson family can be found in the vicinity lends strength to the case. It looks hopeful. Is it safe to set up as having been proved? It is not as strong as the case of Thomas who fitted so perfectly into the family of Cornelius and Thankful. If it is put into the family of Thomas and Mary it should be done with full explanation and subject to removal upon the presentation of evidence that tends to prove that the family belonged in some other section of the family history.

The case of John is clearly not strong enough yet to warrant his family being connected with that of the John known to be the brother of Briggs and Saunders. The only real evidence is the loss of a John and the finding of a John not far from where the first John was lost. The tradition that John of Pennsylvania and Ohio family came from Rhode Island is at this point tradition only, and of no real value in establishing proof. There is reason to believe that these Johns were one and the same, but the case awaits more evidence to prove it.

PROBLEM OF PURPOSELY LOST PEOPLE

The genealogist is sometimes faced with the problem of a member of the family who has deliberately dropped out of the knowledge of his relatives.

Robert Jones lived his life in a Hudson River town, was married and had one son. Robert was a successful business man with no special troubles so far as was known. After the death of his wife, and when his son had grown to manhood, he suddenly sold every thing he possessed and moved away from the town which had been his home for years. Why he did this is not known. He and a brother next older in the family had been very close in their family ties. They had both served in the Union army during the Civil War and had kept in close touch with each other all their lives up to this time. This brother and the son spent much time and money and did everything possible to find the lost brother and father, but without success. He left no forwarding address at the post office; he never wrote again to any member of the family, and although his mother lived in the old home for a number of years he made no apparent attempt to communicate with her and he had no communication with any one with whom he had formerly been associated in business. His loss to the family was the loss of an individual only. No line was lost, and at the time of his disappearance his age was such as to make improbable remarriage and the rearing of other children.

The son married and had one son, but because of unhappy home conditions followed his father's example and suddenly disappeared. Nothing was ever heard from him that could lead to his discovery by the family. He was heard from in Texas working on a railroad, at various times in other parts of the country, but he has never returned to his family or been in communication with any of his relatives. Unlike his father, he was a young man and may have raised another family somewhere.

There has recently been found the history of the family of a man who was lost at the conclusion of the Civil War when he did not return to his home in Massachusetts after having been discharged from service. Through the World War records of his grandsons, which were secured from the files of the War Department in Washington it was found that this Civil War soldier went to Texas where he married and raised a large family of children, who in turn had sizable families which are now scattered over the entire southwest portion of the country.

What mental process prompts a man to drop out of all touch with his home and family is not the business of the genealogist. His problem is to find him again and put him back, on the record at least, in the family circle.

War has always been a medium by which discontented men could lose themselves, and the records of the War Department are helpful in finding some of them. The United States Pension Department also sometimes renders great assistance. The genealogist will have occasion to cultivate the acquaintance of both of these agencies for information.

SHALL PROBLEMS HOLD UP WORK?

The question arises as to how long the publication of the genealogy shall be held up pending the search of such cases and the solution of the many and varied problems that arise. If the book is held from print for this cause it is safe to say that it will never be printed. The genealogist must determine when he has made a reasonable search and not spoil his entire work by unduly waiting to untangle all of these knotty lines. Many of the problems will never be settled beyond a reasonable doubt. The perfect genealogy has never yet been written.

However it is not necessary that the genealogist feel that his work is done when his book goes to print. The author of the Parsons Genealogy, after the printing of his book spent several years in continuation of his search with the result that he published a second volume as large as his first book. This is an admirable thing to do.

It must be remembered that there have been cited but a few of the many dropped line problems that will arise throughout the work. While the book may go to print with many of these problems unsolved, the scent of the chase is in the blood of the genealogist and he cannot drop the search. He will go on hunting in spite of everything. He will find new leads that will uncover rich mines of family history and he will always meet problems which will tax his keenest mental powers.

The subject of Problems has been considered in this chapter largely from the standpoint of genealogy, and their solution, to that extent, will be the united effort of the genealogist and other members of the family effected by the questions involved, while in the Ancestral History they will effect no one especially except the examiner or his client and, because their solution is of no interest to others, it will resolve itself into a lone hunt.

Problems affect the Ancestral History as vitally as they do the Genealogy but their solution or failure of solution has a far different result. In Genealogy it may mean the inclusion or exclusion of a large number of people comprising an entire branch of the family many of whom are still living and vitally interested. In Ancestral History it will determine the continuation of one line of ancestors and the anteceding lines running therefrom. In the former it is an ancestor and his descendants, and in the latter it is an ancestor and his ancestors.

In the genealogy it may delay publication or mean omissions and the time element enters the problem, while in ancestral work there being no question of publication, the matter of time does not become a vital consideration.

Cumulative evidence may be sufficient to convince the examiner that he has discovered his correct line which will produce an unbroken chain of ancestry, but he will find, however, if his aim is to secure admission to some of the better known hereditary societies that only documentary evidence is sufficient to establish his line of blood.

The children of succeeding generations of Thomas and Mary Robinson referred to above may well be included with the descendants of Cornelius and Thankful with a proper recitation of the evidence which leads to the conclusion that they are properly placed in the family, but if Cornelius or Thankful had been a descendant of a "Mayflower" passenger, or if he had seen service in the American Revolution, it would be found that the evidence which admitted the family of Thomas and Mary to the genealogy would not admit their descendants to membership in the hereditary societies basing their lines from "Mayflower" passengers or Revolutionary soldiers. There can be no explanations of evidence in the hereditary societies. The fact of record alone counts.

Many vexing situations will arise in ancestral work. For illustration, in an Ancestral History going back in many lines without interruption into early English families it is discovered that a great-grandmother (which in ancestral work is rather recent history) was Sally Pratt, the first white child born in Halifax, Vermont. There is no town record, gravestone, family Bible or other known means of finding out who Sally's father and mother were, when or from where they came to Halifax. Years of search have been to no avail and the history is stopped in that line with only three known generations back of the examiner. All histories covering towns from which early families emigrated to Halifax have been studied. The origins of other families in the town have been examined. All published Pratt Genealogies (and such a common name as Pratt is a disadvantage) have been scrutinized. In all the places searched there is no hint of Sally. The Ancestral History will proceed along other lines but there will always be a watchful eye for Sally Pratt. She may turn up in some unlooked for place and the problem of years be solved in a minute.

For the ancestral worker these problematical situations soon become the absorbing part of the work. They call for skill and science and demand a lively imagination. They are the real sport of the occupation and because they are of such vital interest to the genealogist they relieve what otherwise would be drudgery and a monotonous task.

IV
Publication

CHAPTER ONE : *INTRODUCTION*

ALL manuscript for publication must be typewritten on one side of the sheet only. This may be done by the compiler or under his direction, or the publisher will attend to it as a part of his work and make his charge accordingly. It is better if the work can be done either by the genealogist or by some one working with him, and the expense is probably no greater. If the manuscript is sent away handwritten, to be typed in the publisher's office there is far greater chance for error than if it is done where the author can see the work as it goes on, catching and correcting any errors that may appear. If the typewritten copy is read by the author he will discover changes that can be made to improve his diction as well as to check for corrections. Punctuation, if improperly placed, may spoil the sense of what the author has written. The misplacing of a comma may change

225

the entire meaning of a sentence. While the author wants it in one place to convey a certain idea, the copyist may mistake the intended meaning, and place the punctuation mark so that it will convey the meaning she thought was intended by the author.

It is always an advantage if the author is able to use the typewriter himself. He can prepare his manuscript for the printer better than can any one else. If he cannot do his own typing there is much to be said in favor of the dictating machine which conveys the intonations of the voice and gives the typest a much clearer idea of the meaning to be conveyed than copying from the author's handwriting.

The final writing of the work will consume considerable time and should be so planned that new material as found may be inserted in its proper place until the very last minute before going to press. There will never be a time in the entire undertaking when new matter does not come in, and it is highly essential that it be inserted, even at the eleventh hour. It is perfectly easy to do this by properly planning the work.

Family Sections

In those families where there were a number of children of the emigrant ancestor it will be found easier if each child is carried forward as a separate unit, and each unit is made a separate section in the published book. If the emigrant ancestor had seven children who grew to maturity, married and had families, there will be found advantages, both in preparing the genealogy, and for the reader in consulting it later, if these seven children each head a section of the book.

Introduction

The members of the family purchasing the book usually know from which branch they descended, and those of one branch are not especially interested in the other branches. If the book is arranged in family sections any member can consult his own section without working through the entire book. For this reason there is much to be said in favor of publishing each family section as a separate volume. There are many members of the family who would pay five dollars for the volume covering their own section who would not feel they could afford to pay fifteen or twenty dollars for the entire work of several sections.

Genealogies are unlike any other book published. They are not gotten out with a primary view of financial gain. Their compilation and publication must be a business proposition, but they should be neither an object of philanthropy nor a scheme for making money. No reputable family wishes or expects to feel that they are not self-respecting enough to pay their just share of producing the history of their family, or to pay for what they get in purchasing it. Nor do they want to feel that they have been used as a medium by which some member of their kin had attempted to build up a lucrative business proposition at the expense of his relatives.

In the distribution of a genealogy there are two points to consider:

First, the breadth of distribution. The work is prepared primarily for the family and as many of the kin as possible should have an opportunity to purchase the book at as moderate a price as is consistent with its actual cost.

Second, publication is dependent on sale. It is necessary to realize financially as much as possible from the sale of the work. Not unlike every other commodity, there is a point of greatest sale price beyond which one cannot go without loss. Small editions are more costly per volume than large editions. Therefore it should be considered how large an edition can be sold that the cost per volume may be reduced to a minimum, and the price fixed accordingly. It is sometimes difficult to determine the demand for a work of this sort. It may be good business policy to have a few hundred volumes, leaving the remainder of the edition unbound and packed away in the flats as the sheets come from the press. They may be bound when and if the sale proves sufficient to need them. Thus the price is reduced to the bare cost of paper used plus the cost of presswork. This does not add unduly to the expense of getting out the edition that is determined as probable sale, and saves trememdously over the plan of printing a second edition if it should be needed.

If a separate volume is printed for each branch of the family the binding cost is the only extra expense, and that cost any printer will assure the genealogist is not large.

It must be borne in mind also that a genealogy, particularly one on the shelf of a library for general use, will have rather severe usage. Many hands will take it from the shelf, flip it back and forth to find the reference wanted, and put it back on the shalf again. Genealogies are not like novels which are read page by page from beginning to end. They are purely books of reference. They are hauled down, the index consulted, opened here, again a hundred pages further on, the index pages turned to a dozen times, then put away, all in a half hour, only to have the same operation repeated by some one else in a short time, day after day. Such wear, even when given by book lovers who handle the volume as carefully as they can, is trying to any binding.

Many genealogies are bound in too large volumes. Before deciding the size of the book, the compiler should examine the published genealogies in any good library. He will note that the smaller volumes, although they are old and have had long usage, are in much better condition than more recently published large and heavy volumes. With this examination in mind he should consult his publisher as to the extra cost of binding two volumes in place of one. Then he is ready to determine the form which his book is to take.

CHAPTER TWO : *PREPARING COPY*

As in the Work Sheet, so in the printer's copy a form is recommended for use. It has the same advantages in the one place as in the other of guarding against omissions and of securing regularity. It places the copy in orderly fashion before the typesetter. He can follow his copy with less liability of mistakes and with greater speed and ease if he can be sure of finding every date in the same place on the page and all the other data arranged the same on every page from the first to the last. The copy should be arranged as the printed book is to appear. The printer must not be expected to do editorial work, and the genealogist should not want any printer tampering with his copy over which he has labored hard and long to get in exactly the form in which he wishes to present it to his readers.

In order that the work may be left open for the insertion of new matter until the last minute before going to press, it is suggested that a separate sheet be used for the data concerning the member of the family under consideration and his marriage, another sheet for recording the issue of the union, and a separate sheet for biography if there is to be anything other than the routine information of education, occupation or profession and military service. In doing this it is possible when the book is being printed to run the extended biography either before family data or after them. While the work is in progress it is easier to follow the form carrying the information of the parents, with the one showing the history of their children. But in the manuscript arranged for the printer it is commonly found that the biography is inserted between the history of the parents and that of the children. This possibly makes for smoother reading. The story of the parents is all told before that of their children is taken up. When separate sheets are used for children and for biography as above recommended, the change of arrangement for the printer is merely a matter of shifting sheets from one position to another.

By having separate sheets for children it is possible to add new names and information of children not found when the sheet was written.

The preparation of copy in this fashion will require a letter size sheet which files in the regular sized binders or in letter folders or envelopes that it may be easily accessible for reference during the progress of the work. Any one of the above filing methods is inexpensive and provides easy access at all times for reference, which is very necessary.

The form for providing data for the member of the family heading the sheet is illustrated on page 240.

Explanation of the Form

Family The space designated Family is designed for use where the main family is being subdivided into branches as above recommended, and would be marked with the given name of the child heading his particular branch, as Joseph, or whatever specific branch of the family was under consideration on the form. If there were seven children of the emigrant ancestor and each branch was to be carried down independently, Joseph being the oldest child, all of the history of the line coming through Joseph would bear his name in the designated space, even though it ran into thousands of pages.

Generation   The generation would be marked 1, 2, 3, etc. as the case might be, counting the emigrant ancestor as the 1st generation, his children as the 2nd generation, etc.

Number   This space is reserved for the final numbering if the progressive plan is adopted as recommended by the New England Historic Genealogical Society, in place of the index plan of Mr. Lincoln as explained heretofore. In adopting the progressive numbering plan this space would be left unused until the work was completed and the numbers would be inserted the last thing before handing the copy to the printer.

Index   This space is provided for indexing the work as it is in process and is designed to use the so-called Lincoln method. In the event that the plan is not carried to the printed book the line should be omitted by the compositor. It is, however, necessary in order that the work may be kept in its proper arrangement during compilation.

Line of Descent   Here should be inserted the complete line of descent from the common ancestor, beginning with the name of the parent of the subject of the sheet, and writing his name and generation, followed by the names and generations of all those in line back to the common ancestor, thus:

Joseph (5), Thomas (4), Thomas (3), John (2), Joseph (1). This shows that the line has come down from Joseph the common ancestor through his son John, father of Thomas, and so on to Joseph in the fifth generation who is father of the subject of the sheet. The order should always be stated with the name of the common ancestor last, rather than the reverse, that the line may be unbroken between the subject and his parent.

REFERENCES

The printed book should always show the references to substantiate the information given. If a birth is found in the vital records of Hanover, Mass., in the References column should be inserted "Hanover VR" etc. By placing references in this manner ease of work both by compiler and compositor will be promoted.

The remainder of the form is sufficiently plain to need no explanation or comment.

The next form should be devoted to children of the family and in working, should be the next sheet unless there is a second marriage of the member under consideration, in which event a second sheet of the printed form above described would be used for this marriage, treating it as directed under the subject of Working Papers.

For the recording of children plain sheets may be used or to keep the work uniform the following form is suggested. The index figures or letters should appear on every sheet and each family should be separately paged as *abdac ad* (2) if a plain sheet is used, or the form filled in if that method is adopted.

Children should be recorded in chronological order if possible, and the date and place of birth. If the child is to be carried to another place in the book for further consideration under a heading of his own, that entry is all that is necessary; but if it is the name of a son who did not marry, or if married, had no children, or if it is the name of a daughter whose name is to be dropped with her marriage, all of the known history of the child, or such as is intended to be preserved until such time as the line is dropped should be recited, as the name is discontinued and will not appear again in the book.

Inasmuch as the data concerning children will vary so widely it is not advisable to use the arrangement shown on the work sheet for recording them.

Nothing but the history of children should be put on pages assigned to that purpose. If there is only one name, and no data other than the name, a sheet should be used for it.

BIOGRAPHY

On a separate blank page, bearing the same Index Letters or Figures should be written any biography of the family, or the family history. Here again as many pages may be used as the occasion demands, placing the same Index Letters or Figures on each page followed by the page number. Nothing but family history should be put on this page, and even if there is but one line of biography, it should always be put on a page by itself and never worked in on pages devoted to the history of the subject and his marriage or that of the children of the family.

Here again a simple form may be employed for the sake of uniformity. Throughout the entire project it must be remembered that paper is cheaper than mistakes. The cost of paper used or of the necessary printing of forms will be far more than offset by the clearness and definiteness of the information which is presented to the printer and may be in some measure offset by the lessened printer's cost when it comes to putting the book into type.

The wording of the form, of course, should not be set up by the compositor when he does his work, and to make clear to him what words on the form are to be ignored by him in composition it is suggested that the form words to be deleted be printed in a different face type from those words which are to appear in the printed record.

Thus it will be seen that every page having to do with an individual member—information of himself, his wife, his children (unless and until carried forward to pages under their own Index Letters), and his biography, will bear the same Index Letters and will be paged as a unit. The history of each member will form an individual booklet which will be arranged in conjunction with the histories of other members of the family according to Index Letters as shown in progression.

The chronological order of births of children cannot always be followed. Many times there will be found a child who has been left out of the record but who should be included in the history of the family. In families widely scattered, where information has to be picked up piecemeal, some children may have been included, numbered and carried along, when it is discovered that there were other children in the family whose birth date preceded those of the children already recorded. To rearrange and renumber at this point in the work, where succeeding generations have been recorded would upset numbers all through the work done on the succeeding generations. This should not be attempted as it gives rise for too much chance for error in renumbering. The dates of birth will enable the reader to properly arrange the children in their order as to birth and age.

Either one of two methods of numbering may be used, as referred to elsewhere in the book. The Index Letters may be retained as in the Lincoln and the Waldo genealogies, or numbers substituted for letters as in the Chapin Genealogy; or the plan recommended by the New England Historic Genealogical Society may be adopted.

The Index Lettering or Numbering has much in its favor, but it requires more thought on the part of the reader. It is a more professional plan, which in the mind of the laymen, who will compose a large percentage of the readers of the book, makes it less desirable. If it is selected for the numbering of the printed book, there is no change needed in the copy as prepared.

If, however, the plan of the New England Historic Genealogical Society is adopted it will be necessary to go through the entire book manuscript and enter in front of the name of each child of the blood, a progressive number. Not the Progressive Number used on the Work Sheets, because in this numbering the progressive or consecutive numbering will replace the Index Letters or Figures and each individual in line must have a number and only one number can be given to each individual.

The plan has been fully explained in Chapter II or Part I under the title Sources of Information, and need not have further explanation here.

It is, briefly, giving the common ancestor the number 1, and adding the next unused number for each person of the blood until the end of the book is reached, using the first number assigned to the child carried forward when he is again picked up later in the work in his own generation.

By this method if it is desirable to back up the line of any particular person it is necessary to look up each generation, stepping back from one to that preceding it, and there is no way of comparing descendants from any specific ancestor as explained by Mr. Lincoln in describing the Index Letter system in his book, elsewhere quoted.

It must be remembered that this system of progressive numbering cannot be put into use until the composition of the manuscript is complete, as having passed a given numbering point there is no method by which new data concerning members coming in late can be inserted. It will be necessary, therefore, to use the Index Letters throughout the editing and arranging, and discard them later if they are not to be used in the printed book. If the progressive plan of numbering is selected, the manuscript may be kept open for additions until within a few days of the time when it is to be handed to the printer. The last operation should be to insert the progressive numbers and cross off on the printer's copy the Index Letters as they will under the progressive numbering system form no part of the printer's work. It should be sufficient to inform the printer to ignore the Index Letters, without having to cross them off of each sheet of copy.

Marking Continued Lines

Some designating mark should be placed against the names of those children who are to be picked up for continuation on later pages of the book. Most publishers use the plus sign (+) for doing this. Not all typewriters have this character, but the asterisk (*) can be used as effectively. There is no designating mark used with those names which are dropped and do not later appear in the book. The fact that they are unmarked signifies that no further information will be found elsewhere concerning them.

Duplicate Copies

With a minimum amount of work a carbon copy can be taken of the typewritten manuscript as prepared for the printer. There are several advantages in doing this. It is good insurance against loss in the mails or elsewhere. Recently an author had the misfortune to have her entire copy lost by the publisher, and the entire book of two hundred pages had to be rewritten. No one intends to be careless and losses seldom occur, but all the apologies of a guilty party cannot replace a lost manuscript, and in the case of a genealogy it would mean months and perhaps years of work to build up and rewrite the book.

The copy which goes through the hands of the employees

of the publishing house will, after it has served its purpose, be a sorry looking manuscript. A good carbon copy is as useful for the operator of a typesetting machine as the original manuscript. This leaves a clean original copy in the hands of the compiler for use in correcting, proofreading etc.

Furthermore, some thought must be given to the subsequent work of the genealogist. If he thinks he is going to stop his search with the printing of his book, he is laboring under a delusion. He has started something in his mind which he cannot dismiss unless he is a professional who considers the printing of the book the end of the job, at which time he dismisses the family from his attention and tackles the next job for which he is to be paid. This is hardly expected to be the case, as by far the greater number of genealogies are written by novices who are members of the family, rather than by professional genealogists outside the ranks of kinship.

If the genealogist is to continue with his search and attempt to keep his work up to date with the changes in family history, there can be no easier or simpler way than to change the color of the ink in his fountain pen or the ribbon on his typewriter and go straight on with his customary sheets.

To continue work on the family history using only the printed book for corrections and additions and as a base for future investigation, even with an interleaved copy, has many and serious disadvantages, all of which are overcome by the retention of the original manuscript and the substitution of the carbon copy for the use of the printer.

The completed manuscript of one member of the family ready for the printer will present the following appearance:

INDEX aba

NAME Dea. Samuel Thompson

LINE OF DESCENT   Samuel (2), Robert (1).

SON (OR DAU.) OF Seargt. Samuel Thompson

AND Lydia Snow

	AUTHORITY
BORN AT Scituate, Mass. ON June 23, 1679	Scituate VR
DIED AT Mansfield, Conn. ON Sept. 14, 1727	Mansfield VR
MARRIED AT Barnstable, Mass. ON Mar. 11, 1712	Barnstable VR

TO Desire Dunham

DAU. (OR SON) OF James Dunham

AND Sophia Cushing

BORN AT Barnstable, Mass. ON Jan. 3, 1680	Barnstable VR
DIED AT Mansfield, Conn. ON Jan. 24, 1738	Cem. Rec.

BURIALS AT Mansfield, Conn.

RESIDENCES Mansfield, Conn.

EDUCATION

OCCUPATIONS AND PROFESSIONS Farmer

MILITARY SERVICE

PUBLIC OFFICES Deacon of the First Church of Mansfield, Conn.

PUBLISHED BY STEPHEN DAYE PRESS, BRATTLEBORO, VT.

FORM NO. 10-A PRINTER'S COPY.

ISSUE OF Dea. Samuel AND Desire (Dunham) Thompson

No.	Children were all born in Conn. as by Mansfield records.
1.	*Samuel, b. Dec. 30, 1713.
2.	Rebecca, b. Apr. 27, 1716; d. 1716.
3.	*Eli., b. Nov. 20, 1717.
4.	Mary, b. Nov. 21, 1719; died unmarried, 1807.
5.	Elizabeth, b. Jan. 18, 1721/2; m. Prince Sherman, Sept. 15, 1742; d. Mar. 10, 1744. No children.
6.	Rebecca, b. Oct. 6, 1724; d. 1724.

NAME Dea. Samuel Thompson

BIOGRAPHY

The First Church in Mansfield, Conn., was organized October
10, 1710, with Eleazer Williams as Pastor, and eight brethren.
Among these eight was Samuel Thompson, who was a deacon of the
church at the time of his death.

"Samuel Thompson of Scituate" purchased land in "Wyndham,"
Conn., in 1705 (Mansfield Land Rec.). Jan. 11, 1708, James Ro
sold a tract in Mansfield "by estimation 130 acres in conside
tion of one yoak of oxen to me delivered by Samuel Thompson"
(Mansfield Land Rec. b. 1, p. 114).

In 1709 he was allowed land on "east side of Nachange Rive
being a part of the fifth allotment on ye crotch and by draugh
ye twelvth choice of ye land layd out in Mansfield according
ye last Voat of ye proprietors" (Mansfield Rec. b. 1, p. 140).

FORM NO. 10-C PRINTER'S COPY. PUBLISHED BY STEPHEN DAYE PRESS, BRATTLEBORO, VT.

Assuming that the numbering plan recommended by the New England Historic Genealogical Society has been adopted for the printed book, and that at the last minute as a conclusion of the editorial work the numbers have been inserted by pen and ink, and the manuscript in the above described form has been handed to the printer, he will proceed to set up the copy, omitting the form phraseology as indicated by the style of type. His galley proof will be in the following form:

110. DEA. SAMUEL THOMPSON

[Samuel (2), Robert (1)]
Son of Seargt Samuel and Lydia (Snow) Thompson, b. at Scituate, Mass., June 23, 1679 (Scituate VR); d. at Mansfield Conn., Sept. 14, 1727 (Mansfield VR). He married at Barnstable, Mass., Mar. 11, 1712, Desire Dunham, daughter of James and Sophia (Cushing) Dunham (Barnstable VR). She was b. at Barnstable Jan. 3, 1680 (Barnstable VR) and d. at Mansfield, Conn. Jan. 24, 1738 (Cem. Rec.)

Dea. Samuel Thompson was a farmer and resided in Mansfield, Conn. where he was deacon of the First Church.

The first church of Mansfield was organized Oct. 10, 1710, with Eleazer Williams as Pastor, and eight brethren. Among these eight was Samuel Thompson, who was a deacon at the time of his death.

"Samuel Thompson of Scituate" purchased land in "Wyndham," Conn. in 1705 (Mansfield Land Records). Jan. 11, 1708, James Ross sold a tract in Mansfield "by estimation 130 acres in consideration of one Yoak of oxen to me delivered by Samuel Thompson" (Mansfield Land Rec. b. 1, p. 114). In 1709 he was allotted land on "east side of Nachange River, being a part of the fifth allotment on ye crotch and by draught ye twelvth choice of ye land layed out in Mansfield according to ye last Voat of ye proprietors" (Mansfield Land Rec. b. 1, p. 140).

There were six children all born in Mansfield as by the records, as follows:

123   *Samuel, b. Dec. 30, 1713.
124   Rebecca, b. Apr. 27, 1716; d. 1716.
125   *Eli, b. Nov. 20, 1717.
126   Mary, b. Nov. 21, 1719; d. unmarried, in 1807.
127   Elizabeth, b. Jan. 18, 1721/2; m. Prince Sherman, Sept. 15, 1742; died Mar. 10, 1744. She had no children.
128   Rebecca, b. Oct. 6, 1724; d. 1724.

It will be observed that the biography is inserted between the data of the subject, Dea. Samuel, and the history of his children, and that two of the children are continued, viz: Samuel and Eli, who will be found later under their numbers 123 and 125.

THE INDEX

Genealogies are sometimes published without an index, in which event any one having occasion to use the book must read until he finds what he seeks. Omitting an index is an abominable practice and should never be done. It is occasioned usually by lack of funds for publication. If funds can be found for printing the manuscript, certainly a little more money may be secured for the printing of the index. In the Ballou Genealogy of over twelve hundred pages, listing about ten thousand persons of the blood, with the normal number of names included by marriage and the in-laws, the index occupies ninety pages. This is perhaps a good average, and will illustrate the point that the inclusion of the index does not add seriously to the cost of the published book. While it may be argued that it is better to publish a genealogy without an index than not to publish it at all, the genealogist's hard work is certainly placed before the public under a tremendous handicap unless he has a complete and carefully made index. It is advised to leave no stone unturned to secure funds necessary for its inclusion, or hold the manuscript until funds are available to publish the work as it should be done.

Sometimes the omission is caused by the added work of making the index, which is a long and tedious task. But if the genealogist shirks in this particular he will pay dearly for his lack of ambition.

The making of an index will consume about as much time as the typing of the manuscript. It can be made as the work progresses, by which method the tediousness is somewhat broken. Its making should follow the progress of the typing, that it may be complete when the manuscript is sent to the printer. Otherwise the publisher must hold his forms a long time between the proof sheets and the final printing.

The genealogist will need an index for reference as he goes on with his compilation, and it should be made just the same as that for the work sheets. The use of the Index Letters or Numbers in place of the Progressive Numbers shown on the Work Sheets will indicate in which department of the work the data will be found.

When the proof sheets are returned from the printer, all that is necessary to do is to go through the index, and with pen and ink, put on the corner of the card, the page number as found in the proof, after which the names may be typed on sheets and the page numbers written after them in the manner found in any good index. By this method the actual time involved in making the index is reduced to a minimum and the printer is not unduly held up with his work of producing the finished book.

The original index on cards is still intact for use in continuation of the work, carrying both the Index Letters or Numbers and the book pages.

The usefulness of the book is greatly enhanced if the index is divided, showing first those names of the blood in one section, and the names of those who married into the family, with the in-laws, in another section. There is also a decided advantage in making an index to towns and cities. This will add somewhat to the work and a little to the cost, but there is no question of its value to those who have occasion to use the book.

CHAPTER THREE : *THE BOOK*

CAREFUL consideration should be given to the material used in making the book. To have spent years, sometimes as many as fifteen or twenty, in the preparation of the manuscript record, only to put it in print on cheap paper and in a cheap binding is poor judgment. It must not be forgotten that it is probably the only record on its subject which will be published for fifty or more years and it should be made to last accordingly. Expense often plays too strong a part in the publication of a genealogy. If it is worth printing at all, it is worth printing well. Some few members of the family may seek cheapness, but the great majority had much rather pay the difference in cost and possess a book they can own with pleasure and look at with pride, than to have a volume which reminds them every time they see the book that they belong to a family which could not afford to leave its history for future generations, as a first class piece of work both in compilation and in publication.

Much thought should be given to the format of the book. There are four divisions in the manufacture of a book; paper, typesetting, presswork and binding. These divisions should be carefully considered before making a decision.

The page size most commonly used is 6 x 9 inches. This size is generally adopted for the reason that it will fit on any library shelf. Therefore the book should be 6 x 9 if it does

247

not contain more than five hundred pages. If the book will print more than that number of pages a slightly larger size should be considered. In this case a book to trim 6½ x 10 inches would be more desirable because the number of pages will be thereby reduced and the book will not be over bulky for its size. If the book is to make a thousand pages, two volumes to trim 6 x 9 inches is strongly recommended.

The sizes suggested will permit the use of standard sizes of paper which can be cut without waste and thereby minimize expense.

Paper The paper selected should have at least 80% rag content and weigh seventy pounds to the ream. It should be antique finish and with a surface that will permit clear, sharp impression when printed. Too much consideration cannot be given to the quality of the paper to be used, as it must last for a great length of time and anything but a high-grade rag content paper will turn brown and lose its strength in a very few years.

Type The size of type should be governed by the number of pages that is desirable to have in the book. If the book will make comparatively few pages, it is better to use a larger size type which will increase the number of pages somewhat.

CASLON 12 point on 15 point body.

There are also many persons taking up this work who have no intention of becoming professional genealogists

CASLON 10 point on 12 point body.

There are also many persons taking up this work who have no intention of becoming professional genealogists or making the study

GARAMOND 12 point on 14 point body.

There are also many persons taking up this work who have no intention of becoming professional genealogists or mak-

GARAMOND 10 point on 12 point body.

There are also many persons taking up this work who have no intention of becoming professional genealogists or making the study a vocation.

For a book of approximately three hundred pages or more the type recommended for supplementary matter, biographies and write-ups for the heads of families should be ten point on twelve point body. Copy of deeds, wills, letters and matter directly quoted may then be set in ten point solid. The children in this case should be listed in eight point solid and footnotes and authorities set in six point solid.

If the book is to trim 6 x 9 inches the type page size should be 4 x 7 inches. If the trim size is to be 6½ x 10 inches, the type page size should be 4½ x 7½ inches.

Machine typesetting is to be preferred as absolutely new type is used for each order; the spacing between words is mechanically perfect, and the cost less.

Presswork The presswork, actual printing, should be carefully done. The margins around the pages should be so made that when the book is printed and trimmed, there is less margin on the binding side than on the outside of the leaf, and the margin at the top the same as the margin on the inside, or binding side, of the leaf. This arrangement of margins will give the page a pleasing appearance.

Ink of the highest grade should be used and should be of proper consistency for the paper used.

Binding The binding must be carefully considered, bearing in mind that the book must remain in good shape for many years after it is made. The signatures, or folded sheets, should be sewed with best linen thread and have double reinforced backs and head bands. The boards for covers should be of best quality and covered with binder cloth or buckram. It is not recommended that leather be used for covers, because if not given great care, leather will deteriorate much sooner than cloth or buckram.

The book should be attractive and dignified in appearance. It is the work of years and should be in such form as to make it servicable for years. Its information and appearance should lend credit both to family and compiler.

CASLON

"This page is set in Caslon ten point on twelve point body, ten point solid, and eight point solid. The Caslon face in these sizes is recommended for a book in which the amount of material must be condensed into as few pages as possible." *Printer's Note.*

110. DEA. SAMUEL THOMPSON
(Samuel (2), Robert (1))

Son of Seargt Samuel and Lydia (Snow) Thompson, b. at Scituate, Mass., June 23, 1679 (Scituate VR); d. at Mansfield, Conn., Sept. 14, 1727 (Mansfield VR). He married at Barnstable, Mass., Mar. 11, 1712, Desire Dunham, daughter of James and Sophia (Cushing) Dunham (Barnstable VR). She was b. at Barnstable Jan. 3, 1680 (Barnstable VR) and d. at Mansfield, Conn., Jan. 24, 1738 (Cem. Rec.).

Dea. Samuel Thompson was a farmer and resided in Mansfield, Conn., where he was deacon of the First Church.

The first church of Mansfield was organized Oct. 10, 1710, with Eleazer Williams as Pastor, and eight brethren. Among these eight was Samuel Thompson, who was a deacon at the time of his death.

"Samuel Thompson of Scituate" purchased land in "Wyndham," Conn., in 1705 (Mansfield Land Records). Jan. 11, 1708, James Ross sold a tract in Mansfield "by estimation 130 acres in consideration of one Yoak of oxen to me delivered by Samuel Thompson" (Mansfield Land Rec. b. 1, p. 114). In 1709 he was allotted land on "east side of Nachange River, being a part of the fifth allotment on ye crotch and by draught ye twelvth choice of ye land layed out in Mansfield according to ye last Voat of ye proprietors" (Mansfield Land Rec. b. 1, p. 140).

There were six children all born in Mansfield as by the records, as follows:
123 *Samuel, b. Dec. 30, 1713.
124 Rebecca, b. Apr. 27, 1716; d. 1716.
125 *Eli, b. Nov. 20, 1717.
126 Mary, b. Nov. 21, 1719; d. unmarried, in 1807.
127 Elizabeth, b. Jan. 18, 1721/2; m. Prince Sherman, Sept. 15, 1742; died Mar. 10, 1744. She had no children.
128 Rebecca, b. Oct. 6, 1724; d. 1724.

GARAMOND

"This page is set in Garamond twelve point on fourteen point body, twelve point solid and ten point solid. Garamond is thinner than most type faces, affording an intermediate step between the average ten and twelve point sizes." PRINTER'S NOTE.

110.   DEA. SAMUEL THOMPSON

(Samuel (2), Robert (1))

Son of Seargt Samuel and Lydia (Snow) Thompson, b. at Scituate, Mass., June 23, 1679 (Scituate VR); d. at Mansfield, Conn., Sept. 14, 1727 (Mansfield VR). He married at Barnstable, Mass., Mar. 11, 1712, Desire Dunham, daughter of James and Sophia (Cushing) Dunham (Barnstable VR). She was b. at Barnstable Jan. 3, 1680 (Barnstable VR) and d. at Mansfield, Conn. Jan. 24, 1738 (Cem. Rec.).

Dea. Samuel Thompson was a farmer and resided in Mansfield, Conn. where he was deacon of the First Church.

The first church of Mansfield, was organized Oct. 10, 1710, with Eleazer Williams as Pastor, and eight brethren. Among these eight was Samuel Thompson, who was a deacon at the time of his death.

"Samuel Thompson of Scituate" purchased land in "Wyndham," Conn. in 1705 (Mansfield Land Records). Jan. 11, 1708, James Ross sold a tract in Mansfield "by estimation 130 acres in consideration of one Yoak of oxen to me delivered by Samuel Thompson" (Mansfield Land Rec. b. 1, p. 114). In 1709 he was allotted land on "east side of Nachange River, being a part of the fifth allotment on ye crotch and by draught ye twelvth choice of ye land layed out in Mansfield according to ye last Voat of ye proprietors" (Mansfield Land Rec. b. 1, p. 140).

There were six children all born in Mansfield as by the records, as follows:

123   *Samuel, b. Dec. 30, 1713.
124   Rebecca, b. Apr. 27, 1716; d. 1716.

CHAPTER FOUR : *QUARTERLIES*

MUCH may be said in favor of the publication of a genealogy in Quarterlies. Very often it is discovered that
years of labor spent in compiling the manuscript of a family
history which has been laid aside unpublished because of
lack of funds with which to pay the printer. A great amount
of work and the expenditure of a considerable sum of money
have come to nought. Valuable information has been gathered
and arranged only to be lost to the use of the family of which
it deals.

These manuscripts, some of them representing years of
work and comprising hundreds of pages, carefully prepared
and full of data that are tremendously needed, are simply
awaiting some means of raising sufficient funds with which
to go to press. Begun perhaps in a small way with no plan
for publication, the work grew to sizable proportions until
the time came when it could be printed and become a valuable addition to genealogical knowledge, but no plan had
been adopted for printing and no funds provided for it until
the project had reached such proportions as to require the
expenditure of a large sum of money—too large to be undertaken, with the result that the matter was dropped, to the
grief of some poor worker who had high hopes to see his work
in print, and unknown to the great mass of the family concerned.

253

It may be treasured by the compiler who has devoted his best years and strength to it but with all the painstaking and careful work, it is practically worthless unless it can be printed.

It may remain out of use until the death of the compiler. Then it may be handed on to some one else who will keep it as it has been kept, or it may be turned over to some historical or genealogical society where it is buried in their files and of use only to the few who have access to the particular society and its library, or, what is a calamity, it may be thrown away as a mass of old worn and soiled papers and the work of years destroyed.

It would amaze any seriously minded person to know the amount of extremely valuable historical and genealogical matter lost in these ways to the student of the subject, and how many years of painstaking labor have proved of little worth.

Publication in Quarterlies provides one outlet for this genealogical material. Many of the leading historical and genealogical societies print in this way and disseminate valuable information. Their plan points the way for the publication of any and all classes of genealogical matter. The scheme is not to be recommended where funds are available for book publication and the work of writing the genealogy has been completed. If manuscript is ready for printing there is nothing else as good as the regular bound book.

DISTRIBUTION OF COSTS

By Quarterly publication cost of printing may be distributed. A genealogy of a thousand pages costing to print perhaps six or seven thousand dollars in the limited edition for which sale could be found, and which would have to sell for from twenty to thirty dollars, might be printed in Quarterly form including in each issue from eighty to one hundred pages of genealogical matter for from one thousand to fifteen hundred dollars per year, and for a genealogical project it is far easier to raise one thousand dollars than it is to secure five thousand dollars.

If the cost can be distributed in a manner to enable the sales of one year to cover the costs of a succeeding year, great progress has been made towards solving one of the vexing problems of publishing genealogies.

DISTRIBUTION OF SALES PRICE

The main object of writing and publishing a genealogy is to distribute the information it contains as widely as possible, especially among members of the subject family. One of the greatest problems in publication is to be able to produce the book for a price that the majority of the family can afford to pay. If, instead of delivering the entire work at one time for a price of from twenty to thirty dollars, the same record may be delivered in instalments of four Quarterlies a year for a price of around four dollars per year the result would be twofold, first, a much larger sale and, second, a wider distribution.

Were there ample funds with which to print a large genealogy in regular bound book form there is little object in doing it if the sale price must be so high as to preclude members of the subject family from purchasing it. It may be possible to raise a sufficient fund to print the book and sell at less than cost, but such cases are not common. If the sale price must be so high as to make purchase possible only to libraries and the wealthier members of the family the project has fallen far short of its greatest usefulness.

There are many more families who can spend four dollars a year over a period of years than can afford to spend twenty dollars at any one time. This is a strong point in favor of Quarterly publication which can be sold at a price to compare with any of the better grade magazines.

It may be found advisable for the same price to print and deliver at one time a yearly volume instead of the four issues of a Quarterly. There will be seen both advantages and disadvantages to the plan. It is a matter which the genealogist may consider.

CORRECTIONS AND ADDITIONS

In every published genealogy there are bound to be many errors and omissions. Wrong dates, incorrect names, a child left out and other items which will develop as soon as the book is off the press and in the hands of the readers. Usually these are errors and omissions for which the genealogist is in no way to blame, but when the book is printed and bound and distributed they have become a part of the record and cannot be rectified. They must stand as printed so long as the book is used.

If, however, the genealogy is printed in sections it is a perfectly easy matter to add an appendix in each volume which may be printed in the last issue of the year, and in which such errors as discovered may be corrected and matter previously omitted may be added. Thus when the sections are all printed and the genealogy is complete it will be much more free from errors and omissions than would be possible under any other plan of printing.

In Quarterly publication an index should be added for each volume which should appear in the final issue of the year. Thus each year's combined issues with index will constitute a volume and it should be clearly marked and treated as one complete volume of a series.

PUBLICATION DURING COMPILATION

Another advantage of Quarterly form of printing is that publication may be commenced at an earlier date than would be possible were the entire genealogy to be written before going to press with any part of the history. There are two advantages which may be gained by commencement of publication while the work of construction is still going on:

First, It is always necessary to create an interest on the part of the family in order that they render the genealogist their co-operation and assistance in gathering data. There is no better way known than to begin to publish and distribute the history, thus keeping before them a regular reminder in the form of the Quarterly. One of the problems of gathering data from the family is the dilatoriness with which members answer queries for information of the kin. If they are brought to the realization that the work is going on the press with regularity and that if they do not do at once what is asked of them they are very likely to have information of their family either omitted entirely or put in an appendix, they will be spurred to quicker action which will prove a great advantage to the genealogist.

Second, Any and all data the compiler has secured and completed should be available for use as soon as possible. It is not uncommon for a period of ten years to elapse between the beginning and the completion of preparation of a genealogy and there is no point in withholding from the public such parts of the work as have been completed. When the genealogist has reached the point in his work where he is certain that he can keep ahead of the printer there is no valid reason why his completed work should not be available for use by the family and the student while the balance of the work is in progress.

Numbering

If the genealogy is to be published in sections it is necessary that the numbering plan adopted be sufficiently flexible to enable the addition of new matter or the revision of old matter without upsetting the general scheme of the work. It will, therefore, be necessary to adopt the lettering plan used and described by Mr. Lincoln in the Lincoln and the Waldo genealogies or its variation with numbers as found in the Chapin genealogy, either of which possesses this feature of elasticity. This plan has been fully explained in other places in the book and needs no further comment. By its use the entire project is kept open for additions, and publication may proceed from any point. If it is desired first to complete the history of those persons and families bearing the family surname, it can be done, going back at some later time to take up and print the record of the families of daughters who married and dropped the ancestral surname for those of their husbands.

There is such a degree of flexibility to the Quarterly publication plan that it may be made to serve any one of a number of laudible family projects and schemes.

THE QUARTERLY

What was said in the preceding chapter entitled "The Book," regarding paper, type and workmanship apply equally to the Quarterly. The publication should be as high grade in one as in the other because the Quarterlies are to become a permanent issue. The time may arrive when it will seem advisable, after the genealogy is completed, to gather up all the data contained in the Quarterly volumes and, after rearrangement bringing into proper sequence and with appendix data in their proper place, all families and members of families, to publish a bound book genealogy in one or more volumes. If this is undertaken, however, there will be a large proportion of the family who, having purchased the Quarterlies and become accustomed to their arrangement, will not care to spend the money necessary to purchase the definitive edition in as much as they would secure nothing new other than a more continuous arrangement. Therefore the Quarterlies will constitute their permanent edition.

The Quarterlies should be uniform in size, not only for the four issues of the year, but from year to year, in order that the purchaser may have them bound in volumes if he so desires. For this reason it is preferable that they be bound with a high-grade paper cover suitable either as a permanent binding or for removal if they are assembled in volumes with a more lasting and expensive cover. The edges should not be trimmed but left rough which will leave the book a little larger than the size recommended for the bound genealogy. When the volume is bound it will be trimmed to size thus producing when it is finished the same general appearance as the tight bound genealogy referred to in the preceding chapter. The printed page size, however, should be the same in both styles of publication.

Something should be said regarding the disposition of genealogical manuscripts for which no funds can be secured for publication. It is to be regretted if a good genealogy cannot be financed for publication, but if it is finally determined that such is the case, the manuscript should not be cast aside. Several of the historical and genealogical societies which have publishing facilities are constantly on the watch for worth-while genealogies which they can present serially in their magazines. While this is not an ideal method of publication as viewed by a genealogist who has spent his time and money in compiling a family history, it is far better than burying the data in oblivion by hoarding them and depriving students of the subject the opportunity of gaining the information they contain.

As a last resort it is recommended that the genealogist get in communication with some good historical society which prints a magazine that has good standing and negotiate for the printing of his manuscript, realizing that any printing is better than no printing at all. In the last analysis the object to be obtained in a genealogy is to gather and disseminate genealogical information and if it cannot be accomplished in the manner most desired, let it proceed in a less desirable way so long as the object is finally achieved.

CHAPTER FIVE : *FINANCING*

THE subject of financing the publication of the genealogy, while placed at the end of this treatise, should be the first matter to be considered. It is a worthy occupation to prepare the history of a family, but if the history is not going to be published, the amount of work and expense involved would scarcely be justified. Before the genealogist actually begins his compilation of facts he must determine what method he, or someone else, is going to employ to give the result of his work to the family and to the public.

PRIVATE PUBLICATION

Many genealogies are printed privately. If the writer has the means and wishes to finance his own publication it is perfectly proper that he do so. Genealogies financed this way are, however, usually brief sections of a main family, being only that branch which covers the writer and his portion of the family. A complete work covering an entire family is ordinarily considered too large a proposition for one person to feel he should finance alone.

The settling of the financial question will determine to a large degree the size of the work to be undertaken. It is useless to prepare a genealogy for which publication funds cannot be secured. If there can be raised only enough money to print a two hundred page book there is no point in going out and gathering data for the printing of which four hundred pages are necessary. If there cannot be found sufficient funds with which to publish an exhaustive compilation of the family history in all its branches, the work must be limited to such branches as can be financed, or the whole family covered to a certain point which will exhaust the available funds. It is an open question, however, if there cannot always be found sufficient capital to print worth-while material. Scarcely anything can be more humiliating than for a genealogist to be obliged to face the fact that sufficient funds cannot be mustered to guarantee his accomplishing the most careful and exhaustive work that lies within his power to do. It must be agreed that much in the nature of family histories is not worth printing, but it requires strong evidence to convince, that really worth-while work, in genealogy or in any other line, cannot find sponsors for its recognition and preservation.

It is not uncommon for some one to appoint himself as a family genealogist and carry the entire project to completion. There was recently published by an old American family a large and expensive genealogy covering, on about a thousand pages, an entire family in America. The work was financed by the family association and compiled by a member of the family who was selected by the association to do the work. Within a year another member of the family at his own expense brought out a genealogy covering a large branch of the same family. While there was no objection to the second work, it was not necessary and if its author had depended upon subscriptions to finance it, he could not have printed his book.

Genealogies as money-makers are never successes. The demand is too limited for a book for which the price must necessarily be high. Because of the composition work, a genealogy is an expensive book to print, and because it treats of a limited subject, the market is correspondingly limited.

If, too, it is suspected by the family that the book is being published with a view of making money, the whole proposition is a failure from the start. A family will not subscribe for its history knowing that some one member is attempting financial gain by its publication.

Publication by a Group

Next to the absolute independence which the genealogist enjoys when he publishes at his own expense, is the plan of securing an underwriting by some group composed of members of the family.

It is entirely possible to get together a few kinsmen who will have a sufficient interest in the project to guarantee the necessary funds for publication, realizing that eventually they will get back some portion of their investment, but that a certain percentage will have to be charged off on their profit and loss accounts to family interest. This plan may be easier for the genealogist than having to deal with the family as a whole.

Unless the genealogist proposes to finance his own work, there should be a very clear-cut and definite business arrangement covering the entire proposition. If the funds for publication are coming from other sources than the genealogist himself, he should not be expected to have any prominent part in the securing of them. The gathering of the data and the preparation of the manuscript are usually labors of love on the part of the genealogist, and are all that should be expected of him regarding the project. Neither the writer nor other members of the family expect it to cost the genealogist real money, but it does cost him years of painstaking labor and time which might be productive of financial gain along other lines of activity. It is ample contribution for the editor to prepare the history with his mind free from the financial cares of its publication.

In making the financial arrangements, whether with a selected group or with the family as a whole, the genealogist should obey the Biblical injunction to sit down and count the cost before he commences his construction. First, he must determine if there is a real need and demand for a family history. While the public may appreciate the book which it may consult in the libraries, the public is not going to be the purchaser. Does the family have sufficient interest in the publication to guarantee their willingness to back the scheme with the money necessary for publication?

Next, the genealogist having satisfied himself that there is a proper demand for the history, he must determine if it is the wish of the family that he become its compiler. There is a vast difference between choosing to write a family genealogy, and being chosen to do the work. The genealogist should beware of a self-appointed task unless he is prepared to be the paymaster.

In counting the cost it should not be forgotten that printing the book is by no means the entire cost involved. There is much expense of postage, stationery, printing, travel, clerk hire where the genealogist cannot search the records himself, and innumerable other ways of spending sums of money in the preparation of the manuscript.

Financing by a Family Association

While it is not the province of this treatise to go into the forming of family associations, that is another method, and the most common one, by which the preparation and publication of a family history can be accomplished. Although the association should, and probably will, include a large membership, it is not necessarily any harder for the genealogist than the group method. If the matter is to become the work of the entire family through a family association a Committee on Records and Publication should be elected to have the entire matter in charge. This committee should be chosen with the greatest care. They are to have the supervision of a very important undertaking involving the expenditure of a considerable sum of money. There should not be over five members of the committee, and three is better, and they should be so situated that they may meet without undue expenditure of time or money. It may be advantageous to the life of the association to have a large board of directors or trustees scattered from Maine to California, but it is fatal to a records and publication committee to be so separated territorially. The committee should be selected for their willingness to put active work into the proposition and with a knowledge of what is to be done and how it is to be accomplished. Election to certain offices in the association tendered members, may be with a view to honor them regardless of whether they do any specific work or not, but on this committee keen interest and ability should mark the selection of its members. The genealogist should always be a member of the committee, either elected or ex-officio, as he must keep in close touch with the committee and they with him and the progress of his work.

There is much to be said in favor of bringing the entire family into the financial arrangements. Assuming that there is a family association, there can be no more laudable cause for its existence and activity than the recording and publishing of its family history. That will furnish a worthy object for the family activities for a number of years. If the genealogy is to be published as a family enterprise it will serve the double purpose of providing funds and awakening interest among the various members of the family. This is very essential for the final distribution of the published book. The genealogist must learn early in his labors that a very important part of his work is to arouse a co-operative spirit in the minds of as many members of the family as possible. Contact should be made with many members of the family. This is absolutely essential for the success of the work. People are not interested in plans in which they have no part. Members of the family must be made to feel their responsibility, both in the preparation and in the publication of the family history. They must be convinced that it is their united business. While the quest for knowledge and information will do much along these lines, there is no method which can be devised which will bring out interest quite so well as financial co-operation. A membership with a small fee attached making one a member of a family association which has under way the preparation of a genealogy will tend to foster that mental attitude of family solidarity which is so essential in all this work.

In a family association where a genealogy is contemplated there should be established a publication fund. This fund should have nothing to do with the operating funds of the association. There will be found many members who will make contributions of various sums if they can be assured that the money so given is set aside for publication purposes only, and does not become a part of the general funds of the association to be spent for its ordinary operating expenses. This fund should be preserved for publication purposes and may or may not include the cost of compilation. The securing of pledges, the seeking of endowments and the general trusteeship of this publication fund should be a vital part of the work of the records and publication committee.

It is no part of the subject of gathering and recording family history to discuss other objectives which might claim the attention of family associations, but, nevertheless, attention should be given by the association to the object of its existence at such time as the genealogy shall have been published. This should enter into the general financing plan as a continuation project. There will come a time when the object of publication reaches its culmination, and the financing of the genealogy is greatly enhanced if there is indicated beyond its publication an open door for the activities of the association. There are many excellent projects which may be worked out to keep alive and healthy a family as a unit of activity. Some determined forward movement should be selected which can be the recipient of such special funds as shall remain after the publication of the family records. By this means the records and publication committee can approach members for financial assistance, guaranteeing them good use of substantial sums of money for generations to come, and making the gathering and preserving of the family history one department of an institution devoted to the highest and truest interests of an American family.

PUBLISHERS

The work of printing the book should be entrusted to some publishing house with experience in the publication of records. There are a number of firms who specialize in bookmaking, as differentiated from other kinds of printing. They have special equipment for doing the work with accuracy and safety. Their proofreaders are experienced in their specialty. Their work may not surpass that of others from the standpoint of general printing, but a specialist in any line of activity has advantage over the general manufacturer, and the publishing of a genealogy is a highly specialized printing operation.

After the genealogist has selected a printer of experience and ability in this line of work, he should take him into his confidence as he would his lawyer or his doctor. He will find by doing this he will save himself unnecessary expense and possible grief after the book has been made.

Index

ABBREVIATIONS, 154.
ADDITIONS and Corrections, 256.
ADDRESSES, Post Office ruling regarding, 70, 71; to be included in the printed genealogy, 152; value of, 176.
ADMINISTRATION papers, information contained in, 53.
AMBIGUITY, 147.
AMERICAN Genealogies and Genealogical Material, cumulative index of, 38.
AMERICAN origin, problem of, 207.
ARMSTRONG's Notable Families, 41.
ANCESTRAL charts, 81; contents of, 17; definition of, 17; illustration of, 83; provision in for unfound lines, 84.
ANCESTRAL History, biography in, 107; chart for children, illustration of, 106; collateral branches, treatment of, 88; definition of, 17; desirability of printing forms for, 87; extent of, 18; form for, 87; form for, illustration of, 103; form for; size of, 80; illustration of pages in, 89, 90; manuscript book of, 80; method of preparing, 82; scope of, 18; starting point of, 18; working papers for, 121; working papers for, illustration of, 122, 123.
ANCESTRAL records, increasing interest in, 13; non-professional interest in, 14; professional interest in, 14; ease of preparing of, 15.
ANCESTRAL research, inexpensiveness of, 15.
ANCIENT records, where found, 54.
APPENDIX, families to be included in the genealogy, 206.
ARNOLD, JAMES N., Vital Records of Rhode Island, 45.
ASSENT, Lines of, 98.
AUSTIN, JOHN OSBORN, Rhode Island Families, 41.
AUTHORITY, how recorded, 158; recording references of, 100, 146; references of, 177.

BACKING up the book, 29.
BACKING up the line, 26, 29.
BIBLES, family, records in, 54, 60.
BINDERS, ring, limitations of, 166; styles of, 85.
BINDING of printed book, 250.
BIOGRAPHY, 176; inclusion of in ancestral history, 88; recording of, 105, 149; business interests in, 110; educational interests in, 107; military record in, 107; political interest in, 110; religious interest in, 110; separate sheets for, 88; what included in, 88; worthless forms of, 150.
BIOGRAPHICAL sketches, 47.
BLOOD line, checked for references of, 174 191.
BOOK, papers to be used in, 248; size of edition of, 228; type to be used in, printing of, 248.
BOOKS, borrowing of, by mail, 50; from libraries, 50.
BOUNDARIES of towns, changes of, 34.
BURKE, BERNARD, Heraldic dictionary of, 48; John, Heraldic dictionary of, 48.
BURIAL places, recording of, 100.
BUSINESS interests, inclusion of in genealogy, 153.

CARBON copies, value of, 58.
CEMETERY records, ambiguity of, 55; dependability of, 55; vital records from, 44.
CENSUS reports, value of, 54.
CHANGES of names of towns, 33.
CHAPIN Genealogy, numbering plan of, 27, 171, 236; advantages of, 27.
CHARACTER, changed views of, 77; study of, 77.
CHARTS, ancestral, contents of, 17; definition of, 17; desirability for, 81; forms of, 81; general requirements of, 81; methods of preparing, 82.
CHILDREN, data of, 179; form for recording of, 164; record of, 104; recording of, 179; in chronological order, 234.
CHURCH records, early vital records in, 44; information from, 51.
CIRCUMSTANTIAL evidence, 203, 206; illustration of, 212ff; value of, 205.
CITY directories, 63.
CLARK's Heraldic dictionary, 48.
CLERKS, Town, information from, 71.
COAT of arms, use of, 70.
COATS of arms, as illustrations, 115.
COLLATERAL relatives, treatment of in ancestral history, 88.
COMPENSATION for assistance, 72.
COMPOSITOR, instructions to, 235.
CONFLICTING data, 176.
CONGRESSIONAL Library, catalog of, 38.
CONNECTICUT families, Hinman's dictionary of, 40.
CONNECTING links, method of finding, 32.
CONTINUATION of investigation after publication, 239.

CONTINUATION sheets, 197; how carried about, 201.
CONTINUED lines, method of marking of, 238.
COPY, preparation of for printer, 231.
CORRECTIONS and additions, 256.
CORRESPONDENCE file, how indexed, 200.
CORRESPONDENCE index, 199.
CORRESPONDENCE material, 160.
COSTS, 265.
COUNTY and state Gazetteers, 46.
COURTS, records of, 47; early, where found, 54; equity, 53.
CROSS indexing, 163.
CROSS references, 194.
CROZIER's Heraldic dictionary, 48.
CUMULATIVE evidence, 203.
CUMULATIVE indexes, 37.
CUMULATIVE Index to American Genealogies and Genealogical Material, 38.
CURATORS of libraries, assistance from, 72.
CURTESY rights, 53.

D. A. R., publications of, 42.
DATA, conflicting, how treated, 158; family, how entered, 70; original, where found, 50.
DATES, method of writing, 156; placing of, 149; variations in, 146; where written, 175.
DAUGHTERS, lost in other family names, 142; recording of, 142; where dropped from record, 141.
DEEDS, Suffolk County, Massachusetts, 47.
DERRIE's Genealogical dictionary, 38.
DIARIES, early records in, 44; information from, 51.
DICTIONARIES, genealogical, 38; Armstrong's Notable Families, 41; Derrie's, 38; Farmer's, 39; Hinman's, 40; Pope's, 40; Savage's, 38; heraldic, 48.
DIRECTORIES, city and town, 63; telephone, 63.
DISTRIBUTION, of genealogies, 227; of publishing costs, 254; of sales price, 255.
DIVISION sheet, 118; record on, 120; uses of, 120.
DOMESTIC irregularities, 153.
DOUBLE Ancestors, 95; numbering of, 96.
DOWER rights, 53.
DROPPED lines, 195; erroneous conclusion regarding, 142; prevailing method of recording of, 141; treatment of, 141.
DROPPED numbers, prohibited use of, 96; treatment of, 96.
DUPLICATION of manuscript, printer's copy, 238.
DUPLICATION of information, 68.

EARLY communication, difficulties of, 211.
EARLY lost lines, problem of, 210.
EARLY records, 136.
EDITION of printed genealogy, size of, 228.
EMIGRANT ancestor, 102, 232.
EMIGRANT ancestors, 138.
EMIGRANT, marriage, problem of, 209.
EMIGRANTS of later date, 204.
EMIGRATION, 137.
ENGLISH ancestry, Marshall's Genealogical dictionary of, 38.
ENGLISH examiners, employment of, 49.
ENGLISH records, how best searched, 49; what they embrace, 49.
ENVELOPES, filing, size of, 210.
EQUITY Court records, value of, 53.
ERRORS and omissions, 52.
ESSEX County, Massachusetts, probates, 47.
ESSEX Institute, genealogical magazine of, 41.
EVIDENCE, circumstantial, 136.

FAMILY, assistance from, 63.
FAMILY associations, 266.
FAMILY Bibles, 60; records in, 54; authenticity of, 54.
FAMILY, connections, established by cumulative evidence, 215ff; history, secured from public documents, 151; information, form letter seeking, 68; how secured, 58, 59; lines, entry of, 119; development of, 144; manuscripts, disposition of, 62; where to be found, 62; responsibility of, 267.
FAMILIES, segregation of bearing same surname, 139.
FARMER's Genealogical dictionary, 39.
FEMALE lines in the genealogy, inclusion or exclusion of, 135.
FIELD working papers, 182; preparation of, 186; illustration of, 186; office copy of, 187.
FILING, numerical, 118; of ancestral records, 120; order of, 118; envelopes, size of, 201; illustration of, 126, 127.
FINANCING, of publication, 262.
FOREIGNERS, adoption of American surnames by, 204.
FORMAT of the published book, 247.
FORMS, ancestral, 87; printed for the genealogy, 159.
FORM letter, 68, 188; for securing family data, 58; illustration of, 58, 68, 188.
FOX-DAVIES' Heraldic dictionary, 49.
FRONTIER towns, lack of records in, 205.

GAZETTEERS, state and county, 46; questionable value of, 46.

Index

GENEALOGICAL dictionaries: Armstrong's southern families, 41; Austin's Rhode Island families, 41; Derrie's American genealogies, 38; Farmer's New England families, 39; Hinman's Connecticut families, 40; Marshall's English ancestry, 38; Pope's Massachusetts pioneers, 40; Savage's New England families, 38; Utah Genealogical Society's, 41.

GENEALOGICAL Indexes, 36; Jacobus', 37; Munsell's, 37.

GENEALOGICAL libraries, 41; mailing privileges of, 50.

GENEALOGICAL magazines: Essex Institute, 41; Mayflower Descendant, 42; New England Historic Genealogical Society Register, 41; New York, Genealogical and Biographical Record, 41; William and Mary College Quarterly, 42; Virginia Magazine, 42.

GENEALOGICAL problems, 202.

GENEALOGICAL research, limitations of published records, 23; connecting links of, 32; classes of, 16.

GENEALOGIES, distribution of, 227; methods of use of, 25, 28; in town histories, 31; how prepared, 36; limitations of, 36; numbering plans of, 25, 28.

GENEALOGIST, Definition of, 21; duties of, 153; self appointed, 263.

GENEALOGY, careful work essential for, 132; common plan of, 20; general plan of, 135; definition of, 19, 20; determination of plan of, 144; distribution of, 227; European foundation for, 135; Extent of, 20; family section of, 226; format of the book, 229; full and complete, 20; legal uses for, 143; limiting publication of, 140; lucidity of, 147; method of procedure in, 19; permanency of, 133; preparing copy for publication of, 230; publication of, 225; purpose of, 20; scope of, 20, 59, 63, 135; size of edition of, 228; size of volume of, 228; where to begin, 137; who interested in, 20.

GENERATION, 232; index lettering of, 170; numbering of, 170; shown on ancestral forms, 91; chart, 82.

GRAVE stones, records, dependability of, 55; lettering of, 56; photographs of, 114; value of records of, 57; misleading information of, 55.

GUIDE to ancestral research, purposes of, 15.

GUIDE cards, index of, 192; colors of, 193; division of, 193.

HANDBOOK of Genealogy, Utah Genealogical Society's, 41.

HANDBOOK of American Genealogy, 58.

HEIRS-AT-LAW, where recited, 53.

HEIRSHIP, value of information of, 143.

HERALDIC dictionaries, Bruke's, Bernard, 48; John, 48; Clark's, 48; Crozier's, 48; Fox-Davies, 49.

HERALDRY, records of, 48.

HEREDITARY societies, 42; requirements for membership in, 233.

HINMAN, ROYAL R., Genealogical dictionary of, 40.

HISTORICAL libraries, mailing privileges of, 50.

HISTORICAL societies, 41; family manuscripts deposited in, 62; libraries of, 41; memberships in, 49; rights of members of, 49.

HISTORY, ancestral, definition of, 17.

HISTORY of ancestry, interest in, 79.

HOMES, photographs of, 114.

ILLUSTRATIONS for ancestral history, 114.

INDEFINITENESS, dangers of, 184.

INDEX, of ancestral history, 117; of correspondence, 199; cumulative, 37; desirability of, 244; how made, 117; in printed books, 232; how made, 245; plan of, 93; of quarterly publications, 257; of reading, 161; value of, 246; work involved in making of, 245.

INDEX cards, 190; illustration of, 190, 191; colors of, 190; methods of recording information on, 190.

INDEX guide cards, 192; colors of, 193.

INDEX, Marshall's English ancestry, 38.

INDEX sheet, records on, 120.

INDEXES, genealogical, 36; Jacobus', 37; Munsell's, 37.

INFORMATION blank, numbering of, 69; illustration of, 59.

INFORMATION, duplication by family correspondence, 68; how to find families interested in imparting, 58; how secured, 58, 59.

INFORMATION sought from public officials, 71.

INFORMATION, sources of, 23; recording of, 101; from church records, 51; from clergymen's diaries, 51; from correspondence, 58; from cumulative indexes and dictionaries, 37; from family Bibles, 51; from family data, 57; from physicians' diaries, 51; from printed genealogies, 25, 28; from librarians, 72; from newspaper query departments, 73; from Pension department files, 221; from public officials, 71; from ship lists, 208; from town histories, 31; from War department files, 221.

INK, use of different colors of, 88, 102, 104, 120, 124; on working sheets, 168; on correspondence lists, 200; printers, 250.

IN-LAWS, value of recording of, 176.

IMPORTANT items, how recorded, 102.

INVENTORIES of estates, information contained in, 112.

IRREGULARITIES, Domestic, 153.

INSTITUTE of American Genealogy, 58.

INTEREST, how created, 257.

JACOBUS, DONALD L., genealogical index, 37.

KIN, next of, where recited, 53.

LAND records, index of, 53.

LEGAL documents, character revealed in, 111.

LEGISLATIVE year-book, use of, 34.

LETTERING, plan of, 27.

LETTERS, how used, 113; old, preservation of, 113; value of, 113.

LIBRARIANS, advise from, 42, 49, 72; assistance from, 72.

LIBRARIES, historical, 50; books borrowable from, 50; non-borrowable books from, 50.

LIBRARY, Congressional, catalog of, 38.

LINCOLN genealogy lettering plan, 27, 171, 236; advantages of, 27, 172.

LINE of assent, 98.

LINE of blood, checking of, 174, 175, 191.

LINE of descent, how stated, 233.

LIST, mailing, methods of securing, 63; value of, 64; telephone, use of, 63.

LOST lines, continuation sheet of, 197; methods of handling, 195; town and state file of, 198.

LOST persons, delaying work for, 221.

MAGAZINES, genealogical, Essex Institute, 41; Mayflower Descendant, 42; New England Historical and Genealogical Register, 41; New York Genealogical and Biographical Record, 41; Virginia Magazine, 42; William and Mary College Quarterly, 42.

MAILING lists, 70; methods of securing, 61, 63; value of, 64.

MAILING privileges of libraries, 50.

MANUSCRIPTS, disposition of, 260; family, disposition of, 62; where found, 62; for publication, requirements for, 225.

MARGIN in the printed book, 250.

MARSHALL'S index of English ancestry, 38.

MASSACHUSETTS, Essex County probates, 47; Genealogical dictionary of, 40; Suffolk County Deeds, 47; vital records of, 43; war records of, 45.

MATERIAL, choice of, 80, 159; quality of, 160; stock sizes of, 85; for printed book, 247.

MAYFLOWER Descendant, 42.

MAYFLOWER Society, publications of, 42.

MEMBERSHIP in historical societies, 49.

MILITARY records, authority for, 150, 151; inclusion of, 150.

MINISTER'S records, 44.

MUNSELL'S Genealogical index, 37.

MUSTER rolls, 54.

MUNICIPAL clerks, assistance from, 71.

NAMES, given, changes in, 45; nicknames, 45; similarity of, 203; derivation of, 135; variations in spelling of, 146.

NAVY, U. S., records of, 46.

NEW England Historic Genealogical Society, library rights from, 50; numbering plan of, 25, 171, 236; publication of vital records of Massachusetts, 43; of Register, 41.

NEW England, genealogical index of, 38, 39.

NEW matter, inclusion of, 226.

NEWSPAPERS, genealogical section in, 73.

NEW York Genealogical and Biographical Record, 41.

NICKNAMES, 45.

NUMBERING, of information blank, 68; plan of, 94; the published genealogy, 232; quarterly publications, 258; system of the Chapin genealogy, 28; working papers, 167; Lincoln genealogy, 27; New England Historic Genealogical Society, 25.

NUMBERS, omitted, 26.

OCCUPATION, recording of, 100.

OMISSIONS, from record, 52.

ORDLINESS of work, necessity for, 80.

PAGING, of the ancestral history, 118; of printers copy, 234; units of work, 97.

PAPER, for printed book, 248; quality of for work, 85.

PENSION Department of the United States, information from, 221; records of, 46.

PERIOD of time, most difficult for securing information regarding, 61.

PERSONAL number, 170.

PHOTOGRAPHS, inclusion of, 114.

PHYSICIANS, early records of, 43.

PLACES of birth, marriage and death, order of writing of, 148, 175.

POPE, CHARLES HENRY, Genealogical dictionary of, 40.

POSTAGE prepayment of, 58, 71, 188.

Post Office Department, regulation of regarding addresses, 70; regulation of regarding reply postage, 188; regulation of regarding mailing of books, 50.

Post-publication, 222.

Prepaid postage, government regulation in reference to, 189.

Printed book, sample page of, 243; spelling names in the index of, 195; numbering plan of, 236.

Printed forms, 159; desirability of, 87; for printer's copy, 230; value of, 58.

Printer's copy, arrangement of sheets of, 230; generation number on, 232; illustration of, 240, 241, 242; index on, 232; line of descent on, 232; number on, 232; paging of, 234; references shown on, 233.

Presswork, 250.

Price, sale, 255.

Private publication, 262.

Probate Court, records of, 47; to be examined, 53.

Problem, of ancestral origin, 207; of early lost lines, 210; of emigrant marriage, 209; of erroneous names on ship lists, 208; of purposely lost people, 219.

Problems, delaying of work because of, 221.

Profession, to be included in biography, 153.

Progressive numbering, 170; of working papers, 167.

Public documents, inclusion of, 151.

Public officials, assistance from, 71.

Public records, arrangement for examination of, 52; examination of, 71; indexes of, 53.

Publication, committee of, 266; during continued compilation, 257; fund for, 268; by group of underwriters, 264; by family association, 266.

Publishers, 269.

Purposely lost people, problem of, 219.

Quarterly publications, 253.

Questionnaire, form of, 65, 66; to whom sent, 64.

Readability, 148.

Reading between the lines, 151, 152.

Reading, index of, 161.

Real estate, value of genealogical record regarding title to, 143.

Recording sources of information, 102.

Records, ancient, where found, 54; English, what they embrace, 49; land, 47; probate court, 47; Essex County, Massachusetts, probates, 47; Suffolk County, Massachusetts, deeds, 47; town, removal of, 34; where to be found, 34; war, 45.

References and authority, 157; method of inserting, 147, 155; in the printed book, 233.

Register of information sought, 70.

Register, New England Historic Genealogical Society's, 41.

Relatives, ancestrally minded, 62; information of, where found, 53.

Reply postage, government regulation regarding, 188.

"Representative Men," biographies of, 47; how prepared, 47.

Residences, recording of, 100; on the page, 149; to be included in the printed book, 152.

Rhode Island, families, Audtins dictionary of, 41.

Rhode Island vital records, 45.

Sale price of book, 255; distribution of, 255.

Savage, James, Genealogical dictionary of, 38.

Secretarial assistance, 255.

Secretaries of States, information from, 51.

Serial publication, methods of, 260.

Ship lists, erroneous names on, 208.

Ship passengers, mistakes in recording of, 210.

Side lines, in ancestral history, 88; how carried out, 88.

Signatures as illustrations, 115.

Slaves, adoption of American names by, 204.

Societies, hereditary, 42.

Southern families, Armstrong's Genealogical dictionary of, 41.

Standardization of materials, desirability of, 161.

State and county Gazetteers, 46.

State archives, early records in, 54.

State lines, shifting of, 34.

States, Secretaries of, information from, 51.

Style of type for the printed book, 251, 252.

Successive marriages, 181.

Suffolk County, Massachusetts, early deeds of, 47.

Surname, changes of, 23, 24; indexing various spellings of, 193; emigrants of same, 137.

Surnames, included in the work undertaken, 135; recording of, 91.

TELEPHONE directories, where found, 63; use of, 63.

TEXT book, contents of, 16; purposes of, 15.

TOWN directories, 63.

TOWN histories, causes of erroneous information in, 33; contents of, 31; date of publication of, 33; genealogies in, 31; how prepared, 36; limitations of, 36; limitations of, 31, 32.

TOWN records, removal of, 34; where to be found, 34.

TOWN and state information blank, 199; how filed, 199.

TOWNS, changes in boundaries of, 34; changes in names of, 33; surrounding, to be searched, 36.

TRADITION, 136; caution regarding, 185; early American, 137; value of, 185.

TRANSCRIPT, Boston Evening, 73.

TYPE, styles of, illustrated, 248.

TYPING, desirability of on manuscript, 86.

TYPEWRITER, advantages of use of, 226.

UNDERWRITING of publication, 264.

UNIFORMITY of work, desirability of, 148, 149.

UNITED States Post Office Department, rulings of, 50, 70, 188.

UTAH Genealogical Society's handbook of genealogy, 41.

VIRGINIA Magazine, 42.

VITAL records, published, authority of, 51; early, how compiled, 44; from minister's diaries, 44; from physicians' diaries, 44; of Massachusetts, 43; of Rhode Island, 45; where found, 44; New England Historic Genealogical Society's work of preservation of, 43; when obligatory to be kept by towns and cities, 43.

WAR department, information from, 221.

WAR records, 45; state publication of, 45.

WILLIAM and Mary College Quarterly, 42.

WILLS, information in, 53; peculiarities of, 112.

WORK, continuation of after publication, 222.

WORKING papers, 121, 162; Continuation sheets of, how filed, 198; form of, 164; illustration of, 122, 123, 165, 169, 178, 180, 182; index of, 189, 191; filing of, 124, 168; method of, 187, 200; method of numbering of, 162; method of use of, 198; method of entering children on, illustrated, 196; size of, 167; illustration of, 165.

YEAR-BOOK, legislative, 34.